To:

....

From:

....

Date:

....

PRAYERS
for an
Anxious
Heart

DEVOTIONAL JOURNAL

PRAYERS
for an
Anxious
Heart

DEVOTIONAL JOURNAL

BARBOUR BOOKS

Scripture quotations marked KJV are taken from the King James Version of the Bible.

Scripture quotations marked AMPC are taken from the Amplified® Bible, Classic Edition © 1954, 1958, 1962, 1964, 1965, 1987 by The Lockman Foundation. Used by permission.

Scripture quotations marked TLB are taken from The Living Bible © 1971. Used by permission of Tyndale House Publishers, Inc. Wheaton, Illinois 60189. All rights reserved.

Scripture quotations marked NKJV are taken from the New King James Version®. Copyright © 1982 by Thomas Nelson, Inc. Used by permission. All rights reserved.

Scripture quotations marked CEV are from the Contemporary English Version, Copyright © 1995 by American Bible Society. Used by permission.

Scripture quotations marked NIV are taken from the HOLY BIBLE, NEW INTERNATIONAL VERSION®. NIV®. Copyright © 1973, 1978, 1984, 2011 by Biblica, Inc.™ Used by permission. All rights reserved worldwide.

Scripture quotations marked ESV are from The Holy Bible, English Standard Version®, copyright © 2001 by Crossway Bibles, a publishing ministry of Good News Publishers. Used by permission. All rights reserved.

Scripture quotations marked NLT are taken from the *Holy Bible.* New Living Translation copyright© 1996, 2004, 2015 by Tyndale House Foundation. Used by permission of Tyndale House Publishers, Inc. Carol Stream, Illinois 60188. All rights reserved.

Scripture quotations marked NCV are taken from the New Century Version of the Bible, copyright © 2005 by Thomas Nelson, Inc. Used by permission. All rights reserved.

Scripture quotations marked MSG are from *THE MESSAGE.* Copyright © by Eugene H. Peterson 1993, 1994, 1995, 1996, 2000, 2001, 2002. Used by permission of NavPress Publishing Group.

Scripture quotations marked NASB are taken from the New American Standard Bible, © 1960, 1962, 1963, 1968, 1971, 1972, 1973, 1975, 1977, 1995 by The Lockman Foundation. Used by permission.

Published by Barbour Books, an imprint of Barbour Publishing, Inc., 1810 Barbour Drive, Uhrichsville, Ohio 44683, www.barbourbooks.com

Our mission is to inspire the world with the life-changing message of the Bible.

Member of the
Evangelical Christian
Publishers Association

Printed in China.

Introduction

We might not like to admit it, but we women
tend to worry. . .and our worries can be so heavy—
and so hard to let go of! But God wants us to release
them to Him. He wants to take away all our anxiety
because He cares so deeply for us. May the prayers
in this book help you give everything to God in
prayer—and at the same time inspire you to
constantly converse with Him, constantly
praise Him, and constantly seek His will.

*Rejoice always, pray continually,
give thanks in all circumstances; for this
is God's will for you in Christ Jesus.*
1 Thessalonians 5:16–18 niv

Give Me Sure Footsteps

*D*ear Lord, I believe You are always aware of me. You know where I am right now, and You have a plan for my future. I want to trust You and be confident that everything is designed to make me more and more like You as I walk through each day. But sometimes it seems as though I'm totally on my own. It feels like I'm facing a mountain I have to climb, with nothing to hold on to. All I see is a steep mass with no way to get to the top.

Show me the path I'm to take, Lord. I trust You to guide me and make a way. When there are boulders along the route, please teach me how to use them as stepping-stones. If I run into slippery places, give me solid footing. When the path twists and turns and I'm not sure which direction to go, I yearn for assurance that You are before me to direct my steps.

It's easy to make my own decisions, only to realize I've gotten into something I can't handle. Remind me always to depend on You to show me every step I should take. Then I can know, even when things are difficult, that You will take me to my destination. Give me grace to believe how much You care about every part of my life. Amen.

A Steadfast Mind

"The steadfast of mind You will keep in perfect peace, because he trusts in You.
Trust in the LORD forever, for in GOD the LORD, we have an everlasting Rock."
ISAIAH 26:3–4 NASB

*L*ord, I confess that often my mind is not "steadfast." More often I am dwelling on concerns over the future, regrets about the past, or the overwhelming tasks of today. I long for that perfect peace that You promise to those who have a steadfast mind. I realize that this peace cannot be achieved by trying harder or attempting to ignore the anxiety-producing aspects of my life. This steadfast peace can only be possible when I learn to rest and trust in You.

There is no one better to put my trust in than You. You are in loving and powerful control of all things that are happening in my life. And You always will be. You are the everlasting Rock on which I can lean for support and stability. You are unchanging, indestructible, and all-powerful. Why would I not put my trust in You?

Lord, thank You that You are there to support and sustain me during difficult and stressful times. Thank You that You are not a God who is far off, but rather a God that invites me to come to You and find security. When my heart is anxious, remind me to run to You, my Rock. Grant me that perfect peace that You promise to those who trust in You. Amen.

When My Heart Is Overwhelmed

From the ends of the earth, I cry to you for help when my heart is overwhelmed. Lead me to the towering rock of safety, for you are my safe refuge, a fortress where my enemies cannot reach me. Let me live forever in your sanctuary, safe beneath the shelter of your wings!
PSALM 61:2–4 NLT

Lord, life happens all the time, and no matter how much I try to plan or prepare for the future, the unexpected occurs. I try to control my world, and just when I think I might have it all together, something happens to remind me that I am not in control. From deep grief to small disappointments, those things can cause my emotions to spin out of control and overwhelm my heart.

When those times come—and they will—lift my chin and help me focus on You. You are a very present help in times of trouble. Only You can calm the storm inside of me when a tornado of uncertainty spins from within. You are my peace and my strength. You provide shelter and safety to my wounded heart. When I look to You, I find a place of rest from all the questions running through my mind.

Thank You for always being there for me when I cry out to You. Thank You for always settling my soul with Your presence. I put my mind on You and I rest in the sanctuary of Your love. Help me live my life under the shelter of Your wings. I close my eyes and rest in You now. Amen.

El Shâma—the God Who Hears

And God heard their groaning, and God remembered his covenant with Abraham,
with Isaac, and with Jacob. God saw the people of Israel—and God knew.
EXODUS 2:24–25 ESV

Greatest of listeners, thank You that You hear us when we call to You. In our simplest joys and through our deepest sorrows, we present our requests to You because You are the only one who has the power to give us what we need and so much more. The troubles of this world grow ever burdensome, but this grace is given to us: we may lift these burdens to You. So here they are. Hear our groaning, Abba! Remember the covenant You made with the patriarchs to enlarge, bless, and protect Your people! Do not forsake us or leave us prey to the devil's sly ways. Though my heart is in anguish, I am able to take courage. You have heard. You remember. You see and You know. You know much more than I do about the state of my heart and of the world around me. You see into the depths of my overwhelmed spirit with the blessed eyes of the Creator, which see the problem much clearer than I. You know the remedy. You delivered Your people from bondage in Egypt. Deliver me from the bondage of sin today. Thank You that through Jesus You provided the rescue. Let me never doubt that, in Your wisdom, You are also acting. Amen.

A Peaceful Heart

*"Peace I leave with you; My peace I give to you; not as the world gives do
I give to you. Do not let your heart be troubled, nor let it be fearful."*
JOHN 14:27 NASB

Lord Jesus, I have allowed fear to enter my heart. Instead of turning to You in my hour of need, I've recoiled in fear of my earthly circumstances. When I consider what You endured on the cross to cover my sin, my grim situation shrinks in comparison. What peace did You have when You demonstrated Your love by dying for me? Yet You have an abundance of peace to share with all of us.

Every day, You remind me of Your peace in many ways. A friend, or even a stranger, will share a smile or a kind word. While stuck in traffic, a bumper sticker on the car in front of me declares Your love to all who will come to You. A tender embrace from a loved one envelops me with the warmth of Your care.

Then I turn back to You, Lord. And in Your Word I find: "the peace of God, which surpasses all comprehension, will guard your hearts and your minds in Christ Jesus" (Philippians 4:7 NASB).

Thank You, gracious Lord, for Your patience when I am troubled, for Your forgiveness when I look away from You, and for Your words of truth to rein me back in with a peaceful heart.

I pray this in Your wonderful name. Amen.

When I Feel Overwhelmed

God arms me with strength, and he makes my way perfect. He makes me as surefooted as a deer, enabling me to stand on mountain heights. He trains my hands for battle; he strengthens my arm to draw a bronze bow. You have given me your shield of victory. Your right hand supports me; your help has made me great. You have made a wide path for my feet to keep them from slipping.
PSALM 18:32–36 NLT

Lord, today weariness strikes me hard, and I say, "I can't; I can't do this anymore." Life overwhelms me sometimes. I have too much to do and too little time. Roadblocks appear from nowhere and bar my way. It's those roadblocks, Lord, that are the hardest. They trap and hold me tight. I struggle to get through them, and while doing so I forget to call on You. I hate that feeling of being on my own, of being separated from You. If only I remembered to stop and listen for Your voice. Then I would hear You whisper, "Yes, *you can!*"

Lord, You are always with me. You give me strength to keep going. When I have my mind fixed on You, I can pass through any obstacle that gets in my way. You are my power and my peace. Whenever I feel overwhelmed, remind me of that. Here is my hand, Lord. Take it. Hold it tight in Yours. Let's move forward together. Amen.

Blessed Beyond Belief

The Lord is near to all who call on him, to all who call on him in truth. He fulfills the desire of those who fear him; he also hears their cry and saves them. The Lord preserves all who love him, but all the wicked he will destroy. My mouth will speak the praise of the Lord, and let all flesh bless his holy name forever and ever.
PSALM 145:18–21 ESV

Be near to me, Father; let Your presence encompass my soul. The nearness of You does me good; apart from You I wither like late autumn vines. It is a comfort to know that You will draw near and You will fulfill not only my needs but my desires. The promises You give are sometimes the only lifeline I have.

More times than I like to admit, I do not praise You, and to be honest, there are only a few times in my life I can recall praising You with my whole being. Lord, I do not live in the knowledge of You. I put a greater score on others' opinions of me than I do on Yours. You made me in Your image, and I am constantly being shaped and molded by Your hands. Help me to be malleable in Your hands when my heart hardens to anything that threatens my comfort zone and selfish desires.

You have blessed me beyond belief. You have granted me freedom through Your Son. May I never stop speaking of You in my life. May I never stop recollecting Your steadfast love and faithfulness. Amen.

The Righteous Cry Out

*The righteous cry out, and the L*ORD* hears them;*
he delivers them from all their troubles.
PSALM 34:17 NIV

*D*ear Father, You promised to hear and deliver the righteous from their troubles, so I guess I have to ask. . .am I righteous? If righteousness means morally good and upright, then no. I'm not righteous, and I have no right to expect You to listen to me or help me in any way. Your Word says in Romans 3:10 that no one is righteous.

Yet, in verses 20–25 of that same chapter, You said that when we believe in Your Son, Jesus Christ, we become righteous in Your eyes. That righteousness isn't because of who we are but because of who Christ is. Because I believe that Jesus is Your Son and have placed my faith in Him as my Savior, You see me as righteous.

So back to that promise, Lord. I am righteous because of my faith in Christ, and You promised to hear me and deliver me from my troubles. It doesn't say I won't have any troubles; if You prevented all my problems, You wouldn't have to deliver me. Right now, I'm in the middle of some deep waters, Lord. But I know You hear my cries, and I know You are coming to my rescue. Please come quickly, Lord. I trust You. Amen.

Sleeping in Peace

I will both lay me down in peace, and sleep: for thou,
Lord, only makest me dwell in safety.
PSALM 4:8 KJV

Lord, why does everything seem worse at night? I feel more anxious about the problems I'm facing. I feel uneasy about what could happen in the dark. It seems the enemy approaches me with thoughts and images to frustrate and torment me when I'm lying in bed. Worries that might not bother me during the day now rise up to mock me. Sometimes they keep me from going to sleep right away.

I know You have everything under control. It's a matter of me letting go of the problems and anxieties and allowing You to handle them for me. Your Word tells me that I'm in the palm of Your hand and nothing can snatch me away. You see everything the same whether it's daytime or nighttime. The darkness doesn't change Your power or ability to take care of me.

Psalm 4:8 tells me I can lie down in peace and sleep because You're going to keep me and my family safe. Thank You for this promise and for peace and safety both day and night. Help me resist the enemy who comes to destroy my peace and disturb my rest. Help me close my ears to his lies. Help me meditate on Your goodness instead of my problems. I rest in You, Lord, because with You I dwell in safety. Amen.

Jesus Is My Refuge

This I declare about the LORD: He alone is my refuge,
my place of safety; he is my God, and I trust him.
PSALM 91:2 NLT

*H*eavenly Father, thank You that I always have a safe refuge in You. Thank You for angelic forces that keep watch and protect me even when I don't realize there could be danger ahead.

Knowing You are never surprised by the events that sometimes turn my universe upside down brings amazing peace. In the world of happy dreams, nothing would ever go wrong. But in that make-believe place I would miss out on the joy of depending on You to get me through those impossible storms.

If we never have problems, we wouldn't need faith. That is an awesome thought! The Bible says, "It is impossible to please God without faith" (Hebrews 11:6 NLT). So I thank You for situations that demand faith—that force me to trust You.

I believe You are continually forming me into the person I need to become, using the circumstances You allow in my life to accomplish Your plan. Please forgive me when I panic instead of running to You, my place of safety. You have shown me over and over how capable and loving You are, to tenderly care for me when I face dire situations. I praise You for who You are and all You do. You are my God, and I will forever trust in You. Amen.

My Good Shepherd

"I am the good shepherd, and I know My own and My own
know Me, even as the Father knows Me and I know
the Father; and I lay down My life for the sheep."
JOHN 10:14–15 NASB

*L*ord, these verses are saturated with so much comfort and hope. There is nothing more affirming than being known *and* loved. I so often fear that both cannot be true—I can't be known and loved. I fear that if I'm known fully, in all my sin, selfishness, and insecurity, I can't possibly be loved. And yet, as one of Your sheep, You say that You *know* me. You don't just know me on a casual level. You know me in the same depth and comprehensiveness with which You know Your Father and He knows You. This is all the more incredible because in the Trinity You and the Father are one. In these verses, You assure me that You know me as well as You know Yourself. There couldn't be a more intimate knowledge.

And yet You love me! Again, this is not just a casual love. You love me with the kind of love that I can hardly comprehend and have experienced nowhere else apart from You. Your love for me drove You to lay down Your life for me when I had done *nothing* for You.

You are my Good Shepherd, and in Your knowledge and love I can rest secure that I am safe, cared for, and valuable. Amen.

To Understand Who I Am to God

I look at your heavens, which you made with your fingers.
I see the moon and stars, which you created. But why are
people even important to you? Why do you take care of
human beings? You made them a little lower than the
angels and crowned them with glory and honor.
PSALM 8:3–5 NCV

God, You knew me before I was ever conceived in my mother's womb. You created me in Your image and gave me a specific purpose for my life. Your love for me will never fail. You are always on my side, cheering me on. You pick me up when I fall and carry me when my strength is gone. I look to the heavens, the earth and all my world. You created all these things to give me pleasure and demonstrate how much You care for me.

Help me today to understand how much You love me and why I matter to You. Your Word says I am created for relationship with You. Help me to know You more. Give me a hunger for worship, a desire for Your Word, and a true compassion for Your people. The more I know You, the more I understand myself. The more I understand who I am in You, the better equipped I am to fulfill my purpose. Thank You for giving me purpose. I hold tight to Your promise to love me for all eternity and to never let me go. Amen.

Chutzpah to Trust

But Moses said to the LORD, "Oh, my Lord, I am not eloquent, either in the past or since you have spoken to your servant, but I am slow of speech and of tongue." Then the LORD said to him, "Who has made man's mouth? Who makes him mute, or deaf, or seeing, or blind? Is it not I, the LORD? Now therefore go, and I will be with your mouth and teach you what you shall speak." But he said, "Oh, my Lord, please send someone else."
EXODUS 4:10–13 ESV

*H*ow is it, God, that I have chutzpah to come and beg, at times claim, things from You and yet I lack all courage when it comes to speaking for a Kingdom-cause? You ask me to go, and I reply with excuses. Was Peter, the funny-accent Galilean, more eloquent? Yet the Spirit spoke to 3,000 hearts through this fisher of men on the day of Pentecost. I am scared, Abba, because I see my inadequacies. However, I forget that You see them too. You actually saw my weaknesses before You brought me to this calling, and You still want to use me in Your plan. Let my anxious fears subside, and continually remind me that I have You, the One who made the mouth, who spoke everything into being, who is speaking in and through me. You promise to teach and to be present. Oh, my Lord, please send me unhindered into Your arms and onward into the world. Amen.

A Petitioning Heart

First of all, then, I urge that entreaties and prayers,
petitions and thanksgivings, be made on behalf of all men,
for kings and all who are in authority, so that we may lead
a tranquil and quiet life in all godliness and dignity.
1 TIMOTHY 2:1–2 NASB

Redeeming Father, our country is plummeting toward moral collapse. We watch, appalled, as men and women we've elected to office succumb to worldly compromises. Yielding their ethical principles to selfish gain, they forgot us and, worse yet, they have forgotten You.

Catastrophic disasters, oppressive terror, deadly epidemics, and senseless wars around the world bring hopelessness. Callous dictators sanction the spread of brutality from one nation to another.

We pray for our leaders and all those in authority, that they will see Your light. Our hearts cry out to You, God, knowing one day every knee shall bow. Hear our entreaties and prayers, our petitions and thanksgivings on behalf of all men, dear Lord. Let them bow to You in worship, and not in shame. As they come to know You, let tranquility, quietness, godliness, and dignity multiply throughout this world.

As we come to You in prayer and supplication with thanksgiving, letting our requests be made known, we put our trust in You, Father. We are grateful for the hope You have given us through Jesus, our risen Savior. For we bring our petitions to You only through the King of kings, Your only begotten Son: Jesus. Amen.

Father, Open My Eyes

*For everything God created is good, and nothing is to
be rejected if it is received with thanksgiving, because it
is consecrated by the word of God and prayer.*
1 TIMOTHY 4:4–5 NIV

*H*eavenly Father, I am a worrier. But You already know that. You know that my mind turns dizzy with worry. *What if?* I ask myself that all the time. *What if this happens, or that?* And God, You know that usually those things that I worry about never happen.

I want my mind to be at peace, to shift from worry to thanksgiving. I want to always dwell on Your goodness. So help me, please. Open my eyes and my heart to all the good things that You do for me.

With every breath I take and every heartbeat, You give me life. You brighten my days with sunshine and laughter. You give me strength to endure hardship, and You give me hope to carry on. Your timing is always perfect. You provide me with everything I need. Lord, You encourage me when I lose faith in myself, and You lift me up when I fall down. How many times have You saved me from evil and I haven't even noticed? Your blessings are as numerous as the stars, some big and bright, others subtle, but always there—if only I open my eyes.

Oh, thank You for filling my thoughts with Your goodness! Thank You, dear Father, for You. Amen.

Clay in the Potter's Hands

"You shall speak all that I command you, and your brother Aaron
shall tell Pharaoh to let the people of Israel go out of his land.
But I will harden Pharaoh's heart, and though I multiply my signs
and wonders in the land of Egypt, Pharaoh will not listen to you."
EXODUS 7:2–4 ESV

Lord, You had Pharaoh's heart and mind in Your hands the entire time. The greatest authority and power the Israelites had known for four hundred years was Pharaoh, and You molded his heart and mind to Your will. How compassionate is Your will that You would inform Moses and Aaron, instruct them exactly as events would occur, and let them in on Your plan. You erase all doubt with Your promises.

Lord, I confess that I do not trust You in many situations. My unbelief has me disobey and disregard Your will. Lord, there are times I do not understand or agree with Your plan. I wonder if Moses and Aaron ever wondered why You would not just soften Pharaoh's heart and speed up the process. There are times I question You, but You are sovereign, as You showed the Israelites in Egypt when You hardened Pharaoh's heart. No one, king or pauper, is outside of Your plan.

You have compassionately, mercifully brought me into Your family, and I am no longer an orphan; I am Your child. Father, forgive me for mistrusting You. I will not always be able to understand, but may I cry out to You for answers rather than seek truth in a sinful and hollow world that feeds me lies. Amen.

He Is Near

The LORD is close to the brokenhearted and
saves those who are crushed in spirit.
PSALM 34:18 NIV

*D*ear Father, are You really close to me right now? I need You to be. My heart feels like it's broken beyond repair. Sometimes I can pinpoint the reason, and other times I just feel shattered and heavy, though I can't really figure out why. But, Lord, I need You. My emotions feel so heavy it's hard to breathe.

Lord, crushed is an accurate description of my spirit. I want to have the joy You promised in Your Word, but it seems out of reach. Stay close to me, Father. Wrap Your Spirit around me and cushion my raw soul. Strengthen me, and help me take small steps to find my way out of this despair, for I know several small steps lead to one big step, and one big step leads to another.

Just point me toward Your peace, Father. Let me know You're near. Whisper words of encouragement, or shout them; just make sure I hear. Let me feel Your presence; let me see evidence of You, Lord. I need to see You, need to feel You. Open my eyes to the ways You are blessing me, Father.

I know You are right here. Thank You for Your promise to be near the brokenhearted. Amen.

The Joy of the Lord

Then he said unto them, Go your way, eat the fat, and drink the sweet,
and send portions unto them for whom nothing is prepared: for this day is
holy unto our Lord: neither be ye sorry; for the joy of the Lord is your strength.
NEHEMIAH 8:10 KJV

Lord, I confess that some days my joy level is low. Things don't seem as bright and cheery to my eyes or mind. The sunshine of yesterday has slipped behind a cloud. It's easy on those days for self-pity to creep into my thoughts and steal my joy. I'm left feeling weak and useless. I feel I have no purpose for the day.

Lord, forgive me for allowing self-pity to enter my mind. Remind me of all the blessings You have given me. As I go through the day, enjoying the blessings Your Word talks about, help me remember this day is holy because You created it. Help me look past the clouds on the horizon. Don't allow sorrow to consume me and keep me from having Your joy no matter what I face.

Help me share with others what You have blessed me with. Help me spread joy instead of sorrow. Thank You for the joy You have provided; it will strengthen me for the days ahead. I pray others will see Your joy in my life and desire it for themselves. Amen.

Clothed in Delight

*But you'll welcome us with open arms when we run for
cover to you. Let the party last all night! Stand guard over
our celebration. You are famous, God, for welcoming
God-seekers, for decking us out in delight.*
PSALM 5:11–12 MSG

Glorious Father, I can't even imagine the eternal celebration You have planned, when all believers from every age, every nation, and every denomination gather together in heaven. You'll welcome us with open arms! The barriers that separate us from one another now will be torn down. Earthly worry, fear, and selfishness will fall away, shredded like dirty rags. We will surely sing and dance with holy abandon and drop our self-centered thoughts.

Help me, Lord, to release any ugly stuff I cling to, or that clings to me. Now. Thank You, Lord, that I don't have to wait until I'm heaven-bound to live in victory and celebration. Give me grace to forgive those whose lives touch mine, who sometimes rub me wrong. I believe You long for us to love one another with Your kind of love right now. So I give every part of myself to You, to mold me into a beautiful person and clothe me in delightful righteousness, ready to celebrate with all Your children.

No matter what happens in my life, I put my confidence in You. I want to rejoice in my relationship with You every day—like a ceaseless party—without allowing circumstances to make me worry and fret. Amen.

Cease Striving

God is our refuge and strength, a very present help in trouble.
Therefore we will not fear, though the earth should change
and though the mountains slip into the heart of the sea. . . .
"Cease striving and know that I am God; I will be exalted
among the nations, I will be exalted in the earth." The LORD
of hosts is with us; the God of Jacob is our stronghold.
PSALM 46:1–2, 10–11 NASB

ord, I am often so overwhelmed by the rapidly changing nature of our world in general and my life in particular. Sometimes things seem so chaotic and out of my control that I wouldn't be surprised if the mountains did slip into the ocean. And yet, Lord, even in that most extreme circumstance, I need not fear, because You are my refuge and strength.

You are "a very present help in trouble." I don't have to wait for You to notice that I need You or get in line to talk with You. You are always present when I come with my fears and anxieties.

You have a plan for this world—to exalt Yourself on earth. Because You are in charge of the past, present, and future, I can *cease striving.* Continually remind me that You are God and that I am not. Help me fully grasp that so I will stop trying to control and worry about the future.

Thank You that You, the Lord that has been faithful since the beginning of time, are with me and are my stronghold. Amen.

My Whole Heart

*I will give thanks to the L*ORD *with my whole heart; I will recount*
all of your wonderful deeds. I will be glad and exult in you;
I will sing praise to your name, O Most High.
PSALM 9:1–2 ESV

*L*ord, distractions in life can be deadly. When I take my eyes off You, I am tempted to look to myself and to others for answers. But the answers I need are best answered by You—my Creator. You know me better than I know myself. You love me more than any other person ever could.

Today I commit all that I am to You. I give You my whole heart. I hold nothing back from You. Come into my heart, and shine the light of Your love into even the darkest corners of my heart. Show me the things in my heart that I have withheld from You. I release to You any desires I have that are contrary to Your plan for my life. I give them up. Bring each of those desires to my mind so that I may let go of them.

Sometimes people can become a distraction. Help me see my relationships as You see them. Help me let go of relationships that can take me down the wrong path—the road not meant for me. As I give You all of me, help me become the person You have always believed I could be. Amen.

This Sort of Obedience

And they went and woke him, saying, "Save us, Lord; we are perishing." And he said to them, "Why are you afraid, O you of little faith?" Then he rose and rebuked the winds and the sea, and there was a great calm. And the men marveled, saying, "What sort of man is this, that even winds and sea obey him?"
MATTHEW 8:25–27 ESV

Master of sea and sky, the storm is raging fiercely around me and within. I am swamped by the waves: financial burdens, broken relationships, health difficulties. Where are You, Lord? I feel as though You are asleep. So I cry out all the louder: "Save me, I am perishing!" Forgive me for forgetting that You who created me, You who formed me, have also redeemed me. As You call me by name and claim me as Yours, so You also call out and rebuke the winds and the sea. You answered my cry, even before I entered these trials. When Your children pass through the waters, You promise You will be with them. The rivers and worries will not overwhelm them because You are sovereign and faithful. Open my eyes to see and to feel You at the helm, to be liberated by Your peace-producing love. Let Your great calm settle over me. When the storms of life threaten to capsize me, remind me from the start what sort of God You are and how even the winds and sea obey You. Amen.

A Heart of Forgiveness

For You, Lord, are good, and ready to forgive,
and abundant in lovingkindness to all who call upon You.
PSALM 86:5 NASB

*H*eavenly Father, thank You for Your everlasting love, forgiveness, and mercy. Wrapped in Your comforting arms, no anxious or bitter thoughts can take us captive. Yet sometimes we wrestle against Your embrace. Rather than give up our anger and resentment, we choose to wallow in our discontent. We seek comfort in the familiar burden of impunity and smugly point accusing fingers at those who have hurt us.

Your Word tells us to surrender the wrath and malice we hold against our enemies. Offering the love and forgiveness to them that You have given to us will deliver us from the anguish that bitterness so readily brings. This struggle is a hard battle to win.

You mercifully remind us to view those who have wronged us through Your eyes—the same eyes through which You looked upon our own sinfulness. They strive against human failings as much as we do. Then we concede the truth: prayer and forgiveness are the keys to unlock the prison of our enraged hearts.

You, Lord, are always ready to forgive, having loved us with an everlasting love. Help us follow Your divine example. Let us bring into captivity every thought in obedience to Christ. Yes, Lord, our forgiving heart lets us rest in the comfort of Your embrace once again.

In Jesus' name we pray. Amen.

An Unselfish Heart

Worry weighs a person down;
an encouraging word cheers a person up.
PROVERBS 12:25 NLT

*D*ear Father, anxiety has made me selfish. It has turned my thoughts inward toward myself and my own doubts. If I've looked outward at all, I've looked outward with desire, with wanting others to fix my anxious heart and take my worries away. I'm sorry, Father. I owe You an apology. I know now that the key to fixing my anxious heart is redirecting my thoughts, turning them outward toward You and toward others.

Thank You for showing me that I am not the only one who feels anxious. The world is a worry-filled place. I have been so fixated on my own concerns that I forget that others are worrying too. My friends, family, coworkers. What is happening in their lives? What do they worry about? I have looked to them for encouragement, but have I encouraged them? They have listened to me talk about my problems and tried to cheer me up. And, too often, I have been so weighed down by my own troubles that I haven't noticed that they might need some cheering up too.

Father, thank You for filling up my heart with Your love. Now, help me share it with others. Give me the wisdom to see when they need encouragement. Teach me to listen and to say the right things. Give me an unselfish heart, dear Lord, a heart that looks toward You. Amen.

Coming as the Rain

"Let us know; let us press on to know the LORD; his going out is sure as the dawn; he will come to us as the showers, as the spring rains that water the earth."
HOSEA 6:3 ESV

*L*ord, my knowledge of You is a pencil tip compared to the earth's surface. You are more vast than the depths of the sea; Your might is terrific and petrifying. Do I live in the knowledge that I am in Your presence at all times? No, I confess that my thoughts and actions are controlled by my own morals, not Yours. I become the center of my world and futilely strive to catch the pieces of my plans as they crumble. Without You there is no anchor, there is no stability to any aspect of life.

The nearness of You does me good; draw near to me, Lord. May Your Word refresh my soul. I thirst for Your presence like a cooling hand on a fevered brow. I hope in Your coming; I trust in Your omnipotence that You hear my cries and know my sorrow. Many times I feel as though I can only confess these struggles internally to You. There seems to be no other brother or sister in Christ whom I can confide in. Lord, if it is Your will, raise up a body of believers who can walk beside me in this struggle, who will pray and fight with me. May I patiently wait for Your call and hope in the showers of promise. Amen.

The Lord Delivers

The righteous person may have many troubles,
but the LORD delivers him from them all.
PSALM 34:19 NIV

*D*ear Father, I don't know where I ever got the idea that if I'm living for You my life will be problem-free. Oh, I understand I'll still lose my keys or have a flat tire now and then. But the major stuff—like cancer and divorce and death of people I love and losing my job—Lord, that stuff is just not supposed to happen.

Oh, I know You never promised that. But still, when I'm doing my best to please You and things keep going from bad to worse, I'm left feeling confused. You say You want me to have joy and peace and abundant life, but all the heartache seems a pretty strange ingredient for abundant life.

Then again, I guess it's all in how I look at it. If my life is always wonderful, I might not appreciate the beauty of it. Sometimes You use cancer to teach the miracle of life. Sometimes You allow a job loss to teach us the freedom of trusting You or to give us the self-confidence that comes from finding another way to make a living. You might even allow divorce or death to draw us closer to You.

No, You never promised a problem-free life. But You did promise never to leave me, not even for a moment. And You promised to deliver me from my troubles, to a place of safety, love, and peace. I trust You, Father, even in my troubles. Amen.

The Lord Will Shine upon You

The LORD bless thee, and keep thee: the LORD make his face shine upon thee, and be gracious unto thee: the LORD lift up his countenance upon thee, and give thee peace.
NUMBERS 6:24–26 KJV

Thank You, Lord, for Your blessings on my life. I realize sometimes I take these benefits for granted. Forgive me, Lord. Where would I be if You hadn't kept me all these years? You've brought me through many trials and temptations, given me strength and grace when I needed it most. How many times have I called on You, asking for Your help? And You answered in Your own way, Your own time, but always when I needed it. Thank You, Lord.

Lord, when I failed to accept Your direction in my life and followed my own whims, You remained faithful, extending mercy when I didn't deserve it, causing Your face to shine upon me, and directing me back to the right path.

Looking back over the years I see many times when You blessed me, kept me, and gave me peace. In hindsight, I see circumstances that could have been disastrous but for Your help. I cannot make it without You, Lord. You have been gracious to me when I deserved nothing. Without You, there is no peace. Help me be grateful for these blessings. Help me keep my eyes on Your face that I might receive the light I need. Amen.

Hold His Hand

"Don't be afraid, for I am with you. Don't be discouraged,
for I am your God. I will strengthen you and help you.
I will hold you up with my victorious right hand. . . .
For I hold you by your right hand—I, the LORD your God.
And I say to you, 'Don't be afraid. I am here to help you.'"
ISAIAH 41:10, 13 NLT

What a comfort, Lord! These verses remind me that, whatever I'm going through, You are there. You hold my right hand and hold me up with *Your* right hand.

I sometimes feel stranded, alone, and terribly frightened. Whether I'm sinking in a pit of debt, despair over a broken relationship, or facing a devastating disease, You are within reach. As I make my way through the sludge of emotions and look to You, You reach out to hold me in Your victorious right hand. I extend my frail right hand to You. That puts me face-to-face with You, the Creator of the universe. I look directly into Your eyes.

Instead of focusing on my trials—the mountains that loom ahead, the angry waves in the ocean—I see Your strength, Your courage, and Your assurance. I can look at my circumstances through You and trust You to take care of things.

I give You my problems. My hands are empty, ready to let You hold me. Thank You that Your righteous right hand is always extended to me. Amen.

I Am Yours

But now, thus says the LORD, your Creator, O Jacob, and He who formed you,
O Israel, "Do not fear, for I have redeemed you; I have called you by name;
you are Mine! When you pass through the waters, I will be with you;
and through the rivers, they will not overflow you. When you walk
through the fire, you will not be scorched, nor will the flame burn you."
ISAIAH 43:1–2 NASB

*L*ord, I often feel like I am passing through a river where I can barely touch the bottom and every wave threatens to take me under. And I am no stranger to the feeling that I am going through a fiery trial where I'm sure to be burned. But You promise me in these verses that You will be with me through any trial. You will not allow the waters to flow over me or the flame to burn me. What an amazing comfort that You, the Creator of the universe, walk with me through this life to lift me up over the waves and protect me from the threatening flames.

You have called me by name to be Yours. For someone to know my name means that I have been noticed and remembered. Among the billions of people in this world, You know me *by name*. And You call me by that name to be Yours. What an intimate and humbling thought.

As one who belongs to You and who You have redeemed, I certainly do not have any need to fear. Amen.

He's All I Need

*And this same God who takes care of me will
supply all your needs from his glorious riches,
which have been given to us in Christ Jesus.*
PHILIPPIANS 4:19 NLT

*H*eavenly Father, sometimes life is too full. It becomes a river that has received too much rain too quickly. It moves at such a swift speed, and I find myself being carried away in the rapids of life. Forgive me for trying to figure things out on my own, trying to save myself. I often try to answer my own questions and solve my own problems when, in fact, You had the right answer for me all the time. I also look to others to speak into my life, seeking their wisdom and approval, asking them what they think before asking You.

You should be the one I go to for direction. You know who I am and what I need in every single situation. Help me always run to you—especially when I find myself in rough water. Give me wisdom and understanding. Help me discern what is good and right for my life. Set the path before me. Speak to me and tell me the way to go. Your Word promises that You will guide me in all my ways and provide for my every need. Sometimes what I need most is just to spend time with You, learning to recognize Your voice and then responding in obedience. Thank You for being all I need. Amen.

Every Good Gift

*If any of you lacks wisdom, let him ask God, who gives
generously to all without reproach, and it will be
given him. But let him ask in faith, with no doubting.*

JAMES 1:5–6 ESV

Abba, what direction should I take? What words do I say? How should I invest my time? I need wisdom, Lord! Solomon knew that humans can only experience lasting peace when guided by Your wisdom. I too beg You for this divine discernment. How much time should I dedicate to church ministries? How do I present the Gospel naturally to my dear friends who do not know You? How do I serve the poor without creating dependence and doing more harm? How do You want me to show my love of You and Your love to the world today? My heart is overwhelmed. But I come to You knowing that You will give me this precious gift of wisdom. You do not reproach me for asking but delight in the fact that I am petitioning You. Thank You that You give generously, above what I ask or can even imagine. But purify my asking so that it is in all faith, with no doubt or anxiousness. Let me ask with complete thankfulness in anticipation of seeing You work out Your wisdom through my weakness. Thank You, Father, that Jesus is the embodiment of all wisdom and that through the Spirit His presence is with me, giving the answers to guide through my dilemmas. Amen.

A Believing Heart

"Do not let your heart be troubled;
believe in God, believe also in Me."
JOHN 14:1 NASB

Gracious God, too often we seek answers from our government agencies when distress overwhelms us. The officials who set up the multitude of public assistance programs thought they would help. But they lack the wisdom only You can offer. Often they create more anguish for the struggling applicants who complete numerous forms. They expect the government to provide a solution, and they wait for an answer. And wait. And wait. And wait. Disappointment often follows.

Remind us to reach out to You in faith. For it is better to take refuge in You than to trust in mankind—or his bureaucracies. Let us see You, Lord, in every direction we turn for help.

Help us emulate Peter, who walked on the sea toward Christ. The moment he took his eyes off Jesus, he began to sink. Like Peter, we too plunge deeper into the crashing waves of our personal storms when we focus on earthly provisions.

Strengthen our faith, Father God, when we falter and sink into the gloom of our own making.

Peter cried out to Jesus, and He saved him. You hear our prayers, dear Father, when we cry out to You in despair. Only You can save us.

When we believe in You, disappointment fades in the light of our faith. When we trust in Your answers, our hearts will no longer be troubled. Amen.

A Bedtime Prayer

"The LORD will fight for you;
you need only to be still."
EXODUS 14:14 NIV

*L*ord, when I lie down to sleep at night, my mind becomes a tangled mess of thoughts. Anxiety grows inside me all day long, lurking in silence. When I lie down to sleep, it attacks, and I can't stop the thinking. I lie in my bed reviewing my troubles and trying to solve them in my head.

Lord, I need You. Please give me peace, and quiet my thoughts. I can't do it all by myself. I need You. All this thinking does me no good. It robs me of sleep and pulls me far from You. It leads me down a dark, dreary path.

In my heart, I know that You will fight for me. You are the One in control. You know where I have been, where I am right now, and where I am going. You have it all planned out. So I need to be still. I need to remember that You are God Almighty. You love me. You will not let me fall.

When I close my eyes to sleep, fill my thoughts with Your Word. Set my mind on Jesus, Your Son. Reveal His presence all around me. Remind me that He protects me all through the night and never leaves my bedside. Help me rest in Christ's love and be still. Give me sweet peace, dear Lord. Amen.

Creation

*"Where were you when I laid the foundation of the earth? Tell me, if you have
understanding. Who determined its measurements—surely you know! Or who
stretched the line upon it? On what were its bases sunk, or who laid its cornerstone,
when the morning stars sang together and all the sons of God shouted for joy?
Or who shut in the sea with doors when it burst out from the womb, when I made
clouds its garment and thick darkness its swaddling band, and prescribed limits for it
and set bars and doors, and said, 'Thus far shall you come, and no farther, and here
shall your proud waves be stayed'? Have you commanded the morning since your
days began, and caused the dawn to know its place, that it might take hold of the
skirts of the earth, and the wicked be shaken out of it?"*

JOB 38:4–13 ESV

No, Lord. I have not commanded the morning to rise or the waves to cease crashing.
My eyes have not seen the foundations of the earth, nor have my ears heard the
morning stars' song. And yet, Lord, I selfishly believe my knowledge and plan to be greater
than Yours. Forgive me for forgetting Your power, might, and majesty, for putting You in
a box and only turning to You when I need comfort.

It humbles me to know that the God who orchestrates the universe's symphony delights
in the simpler tune of my life. Thank You for redeeming my life; thank You for pulling my
heart back to You, regardless of the pain. Lord, grant me wisdom and strength when the
storms prevail to cry out to You, the One who commands the waves.

Apple of His Eye

Keep me as the apple of your eye;
hide me in the shadow of your wings.
PSALM 17:8 NIV

Dear Father, the phrase "apple of your eye" means "something or someone that one cherishes above all others." David knew that You cherished him. He knew this because he loved You so deeply and he felt Your love in return. This verse was written at a time of distress, and he begged You to keep him as Your cherished one.

Father, I want to be the apple of Your eye too. I love You, and I want to please You. I long to feel Your presence. I want to curl up in Your lap, hide my face in Your neck, and rest.

I know You love me, Father, but sometimes, when life gets hard or scary or too much, it seems like You've forgotten me. But I know my feelings are not facts and they can be misleading. In these times, remind me of the facts: You love me, and You paid a great price for me. You promised never to leave me or turn Your back on me. And You promised that good things await for those who love You.

Keep me as the apple of Your eye, Lord. Hide me, today and every day, in the shadow of Your wings. Amen.

God Brings Contentment

*Not that I speak in respect of want: for I have learned,
in whatsoever state I am, therewith to be content.
I know both how to be abased, and I know how to abound:
every where and in all things I am instructed both to be full
and to be hungry, both to abound and to suffer need.*

PHILIPPIANS 4:11–12 KJV

My heart is full of gratitude, Lord, for all You've done for me. I have so much to be thankful for. I remember a time when I didn't have money for food, but You provided. You spoke to someone's heart and they obeyed, giving me help I desperately needed. It made me realize that, with You, I will never be in need for long.

Lord, there was a time when I had very few clothes. In fact, I wore the same thing to church every Sunday for months. But now I have more than I need. Thank You, Lord—not because I need a closet full of clothes to be happy, but because You've blessed me financially through the years.

Thank You, Lord, for teaching me that, with You, I don't have to worry about necessities. I can be content in whatever state I find myself, knowing You will provide for me those things that are necessary. I lift my heart and my hands in worship to You for Your provision. Lord, help me always to be content with what I have instead of grumbling because I don't have more. Amen.

Have I Loved?

*Who has believed what he has heard from us? And to
whom has the arm of the LORD been revealed? For he
grew up before him like a young plant, and like a root out
of dry ground; he had no form or majesty that we should
look at him, and no beauty that we should desire him.*

ISAIAH 53:1–2 ESV

*H*ave I ever desired You, Lord, or have I desired what You do for me? This is a hard question, but one I need to search. My desire to know You has become a side job. Loving You has not been my goal. I have only been seeking the benefits of knowing You, not the relationship. Father, if it is Your will, show me my blindness; remove the scales from my eyes and plant in me an insatiable thirst to know and love You.

I grow easily offended, I treat quiet times as an inconvenience, I am critical toward others, and I am only interested in the usefulness of Jesus. This selfish mind-set and heart scares me. Lord, forgive me, though I do not deserve forgiveness. You are a great, just, and merciful God who sent hope into the world. There is no other story more powerful or humbling than the Gospel. I pray that I find beauty in Christ—beauty in Himself and not in what He does for me. Lord, I pray that You become my ultimate goal and the wonderful effects of loving You come second. Thank You for Your Son, Your Spirit on this earth, and communion with You. Amen.

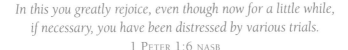

An Enduring Heart

In this you greatly rejoice, even though now for a little while,
if necessary, you have been distressed by various trials.
1 Peter 1:6 NASB

*M*y gracious Lord, I often ask what reason I have to rejoice when I am distressed by various trials. You remind me clearly through Your Word. I am born again to a living hope through the resurrection of Jesus Christ from the dead (1 Peter 1:3). Knowing I am secure in Your promise of my heavenly inheritance helps diminish my anxiousness.

But I still struggle in my efforts to count it all joy when trials come upon me. Worry creeps in to spread doubt. Help me remember that trying to endure these ordeals without You by my side produces more uncertainty. I need to rely more on You and less on my own feeble attempts to resolve distressing situations.

In James 5:11 (NASB), I read, "We count those blessed who endured. You have heard of the endurance of Job and have seen the outcome of the Lord's dealings, that the Lord is full of compassion and is merciful." Job's faith and moral integrity withstood tragedy upon tragedy. You were full of compassion and mercy for him, and offer the same kindheartedness to me as well.

You are always there, waiting for me to turn to You. Each test, which produces endurance, strengthens my faith in You. I can endure as long as I have You next to me. Now that gives me reason to rejoice! Amen.

Jesus' Hands

"See, I have engraved you on the palms of my hands;
your walls are ever before me."
ISAIAH 49:16 NIV

*P*recious Lord, I know this scripture is directed to the people of Zion, but I believe it is also for all of us who trust in You. In Isaiah's day, they thought You had forsaken them, but the prophet spoke the words You gave him, to remind them—and me—how impossible that would be.

Verse 15 says that even though a woman might forget her baby, You will never forget me! I can't imagine any mother forgetting her own child. You must have said that to show us how impossible it would be for You to forget us.

I can do nothing but bow before You in awe and worship when I think about how amazing this is; You've engraved my name in the palms of Your hands. Lord Jesus, when You were crucified, with nails driven into Your palms, You remembered everyone who would ever turn to You. The scars on Your hands are a continual reminder of how much You care. Each time I think of what You endured, I remember Your indescribable love for me and that You will never forget me. It's more than my mind can comprehend, but my heart swells in adoration.

I don't know the words to thank You for such amazing love, but I open myself up to You, trusting that Your name will be eternally inscribed on my life. Amen.

My God Will Hear Me

But as for me, I will watch expectantly for the Lord;
I will wait for the God of my salvation. My God will hear me.
MICAH 7:7 NASB

*L*ord, thank You that You have given us such good examples in Your Word of people who have followed You faithfully. Help me emulate the confidence and trust that Micah has in You in this verse.

Lord, just like Micah, may I watch expectantly for You. You are all-powerful and capable of miracles beyond my imaginings. When I pray, let it not be just because I know that I'm supposed to bring my concerns and desires to You. Instead, let my prayers be expectant, waiting and hopeful to see what wonders You will perform as the almighty God. May my prayers be saturated in the knowledge that You not only care for me, but that You have the power and desire to act.

Grant me the patience that Micah has here to wait for You. In my fast-paced life, I get frustrated when things are not accomplished quickly or when my prayers do not receive immediate answers. Teach me to worship and honor You even as I wait and watch for You. Keep me from the anxiety that so often comes with waiting. Instead, may I, like Micah, trust in Your faithfulness so that I can say, with the same rock-solid confidence, "My God will hear me." Amen.

Hold On to Hope

There was no hope that Abraham would have children.
But Abraham believed God and continued hoping, and so
he became the father of many nations. As God told him,
"Your descendants also will be too many to count."
ROMANS 4:18 NCV

God, I have a dream in my heart and You sealed it with a promise. I have thought about it, prayed about it, and continue to hold on to hope. Forgive me when my hope wanes and I grow tired of holding on. Your Word is true, and I really want to trust You, but some days it can be hard. The waiting is difficult, and You know my patience is less than I'd like it to be.

Your joy is my strength. As I worship You and express my joy for Your goodness, help me grow in my trust for things to happen just as You have promised. It may not come together as I have imagined. It might not look like what I think it should, but it will be more than I can ask or think. You are good and all Your promises are good. I am determined. As I encourage myself in Your Word, I will hold on to hope. For what You have promised will be delivered in Your perfect time. I will wait for it. I trust You to bring that dream to reality. Amen.

Of Ravens and Lilies

*And he said to his disciples, "Therefore I tell you, do not
be anxious about your life, what you will eat, nor about
your body, what you will put on. For life is more than
food, and the body more than clothing."*
LUKE 12:22–23 ESV

*A*bba, I come to give You all my anxieties about the future. All my material needs are met and yet, when things at work get rough, when pays are cut or when there are layoffs, I start to panic. I still worry about where my next meal will come from or how I will keep my family warm. And You answer in Your usual surprising way. You tell me to look to the ravens. Am I not supposed to work or responsibly look to the future? No, forgive my resentful answer. The ravens do so little and yet You still provide for them. How much more will You provide for me, Your child. My anxiousness will not magically produce more time, money, food, or clothes. Release me of this burdensome worry. Thank You for Grandpa Vanderhof's reminder in the film *You Can't Take It with You*. When he asked who takes care of him, his reply is "the same One that takes care of the lilies of the field." Let me seek first Your will and, like the ravens and the lilies, leave all to You. Through this pursuit, everything will fall into place because You, Abba, know what I need. Amen.

A Revived Heart

Will You not Yourself revive us again,
that Your people may rejoice in You?
PSALM 85:6 NASB

Sustaining Father, our hearts wilt like flowers starved for water when hard circumstances overwhelm us. It's easy for us to get lost in the wilderness of worry. Help us remember to come to You to bolster our weakened spirits. "For with You is the fountain of life; in Your light we see light" (Psalm 36:9 NASB). Let the darkness around us be dismayed by Your radiant power.

You have covered us with Your divine love and sustained us with Your steadfast resolve. In partaking of Your wellspring of living water, we are upheld in Your amazing strength. You give us profound courage to persevere in a spirit eager to do Your will.

We praise You, O God, in the assurance that You hear our prayers. "Truth springs from the earth, and righteousness looks down from heaven" (Psalm 85:11 NASB). We can be confident that Your answers will flow to us like a nourishing stream. Through Your restorative power, we can rejoice in You. Then our anxious thoughts no longer have power over us. Those ugly struggles shrink back in the light of Your righteousness and eternal glory to become minor, manageable annoyances.

Restored, sustained, and joyful. . .these three blessings from You revive our hearts, allowing the fragrant flowers of Your resilience to bloom within us again.

In the precious name of the one and only Savior, Jesus, amen.

Anxiously Awaiting Tomorrow

*"Therefore do not worry about tomorrow, for tomorrow will
worry about itself. Each day has enough trouble of its own."*
MATTHEW 6:34 NIV

Tomorrow is an important day for me, Father. You know that. You know the plans that I have and all my concerns. I wonder, will tomorrow turn out okay? Will tomorrow be just as I've planned, or will it hold surprises? I don't like surprises, but You already know that.

I dwell on things. I play them through in my head, and I worry. If only I could know tomorrow today. If only I could keep my mind fixed on a good tomorrow and leave the rest up to You—but You know how I am. I envision what could go wrong, and I worry how to fix it. I make sure that I am prepared. Always prepared.

Jesus said, "Don't worry about tomorrow." But that is easier said than done. That's why I need You today, Father. I need You to teach me how not to worry. I know that tomorrow belongs to You. Tomorrow is not about my plan, but Yours. It is all about putting my faith and my trust in You and believing that You will help me.

So today, right now, I give You my tomorrow. I give it to You with all my plans and worries and all my faith and trust. Take my tomorrow, dear heavenly Father. Take it and give me rest. Amen.

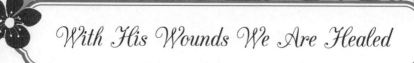

With His Wounds We Are Healed

But he was pierced for our transgressions; he was crushed for our iniquities;
upon him was the chastisement that brought us peace, and with his wounds
we are healed. All we like sheep have gone astray; we have turned—every one—
to his own way; and the LORD has laid on him the iniquity of us all.
ISAIAH 53:5–6 ESV

Father, You possess numerous characteristics that I disregard when reading Your Word. Like a straying sheep, I have wandered far from Your presence and deep into hopelessness and anxiety. Each time, You seek me in the wilderness and relentlessly pursue me until I am safe with You. Thank You for rescuing me, and forgive me for wandering. You came to this degraded and wrecked earth to take all the sin—lies, anger, murder, hatred—upon Yourself. Your sacrifice is overwhelming and awesome. The life, death, and resurrection of Your Son was never a surprise; it was always Your plan.

Father, You have never left us hopeless; from the Old Testament prophecies to Jesus' resurrection, You have always revealed Your plan. Forgive me for taking Your plan, hope, and majesty for granted. The God of the universe inclines His ear to me, a sinner. Humble me, Lord; I wake each day in the false belief that the world revolves around me. Help me live in the steadfast knowledge of Your abundant grace and my helplessness. You are the only Savior, and You are my only hope in these dark hours. I hope in You. Amen.

I Trust You

*D*ear Father, this is such a nice verse to display on a plaque on the wall. But when it comes to believing the words, it's a little harder. I'm good at casting my cares on You. I pray, I lay them at Your feet, I pour out my heart. Then I take them right back. I hold on to my cares and nurse them. I fret and worry and try to figure out how to handle the difficult things in my life. I guess, when it comes right down to it, I don't really trust that You are working. I don't really believe that You'll take care of me.

But, Father, I know all Your words are true. Even when I don't see You working, I can be sure You're busy taking care of things, bringing all things together in a beautiful way. When I let You handle my problems, I'm confident I won't be disappointed. I just need to trust Your timing. I want everything to be fixed right here, right now, but I know You're not just slapping a bandage on my issues. You're handling things in an intricate, beautiful way, and that takes time.

When I feel anxious today, Father, remind me to say these words again and again: I trust You. Amen.

Trust God to Keep You

And of this gospel I was appointed a herald and an apostle and a teacher.
That is why I am suffering as I am. Yet this is no cause for shame,
because I know whom I have believed, and am convinced that he
is able to guard what I have entrusted to him until that day.

2 TIMOTHY 1:11–12 NIV

Lord, thank You for Your keeping power and Your commitment to those who love You. In a world where commitment and loyalty are not important, it's wonderful to know You will never betray us. You remain faithful in every situation.

I know that Your servant Paul suffered many things for his commitment to You, but he knew in whom he had believed and wasn't afraid to trust You with his very life. Lord, we have nothing to be ashamed of by serving You. Help us realize that, as we believe in You, we don't have to worry You might forget us or hold past sins against us. Whatever we have entrusted You with, You will guard it without fail. Your faithfulness is so great toward us.

I pray for all Christians everywhere that we will have the same confidence in You that Paul did. Give us the courage to take the same stand, knowing that You will always be there for us. Even if we suffer for our walk with You, embolden us by Your Spirit to entrust You with our very lives. Amen.

Joy Unending

"Don't be sad! This is a special day for the LORD,
and he will make you happy and strong."
NEHEMIAH 8:10 CEV

Even when life seems confusing and uncertain, I know in the deepest part of my heart that You are who You say You are, and will do what You say You'll do. Thank You for that assurance. I believe my strength and joy come from You, Lord. I can depend on You when I face trials. You will turn bleak, heartbreaking times into opportunities to grow strong and happy.

Storms come. Problems pop up like weeds. Doubt and fear try to destroy my faith, but I yearn to put my hope in You and stand firmly against the evil one who wants to destroy me. Dear Lord, sometimes it's almost impossible to keep my eyes on You instead of my problems. I might say I'm able to face whatever happens, but I can't fool You. Please give me the assurance that, as I look to You, I will be strong and receive the peace You long to give. Thank You for always being there, ever ready to take me in Your arms of love.

Your power is boundless. Difficulties that seem immense to me are mere crumbs to be brushed away from Your perspective. You are ready with the perfect miracle to make every necessary change—in me or in my situation—as soon as I turn to You. I will sing praises to You! Amen.

Unchanging Love

Who is a God like You, who pardons iniquity and passes over the rebellious act of the remnant of His possession? He does not retain His anger forever, because He delights in unchanging love. He will again have compassion on us; He will tread our iniquities under foot. Yes, You will cast all their sins into the depths of the sea.

MICAH 7:18–19 NASB

*L*ord, I carry such guilt and anxiety over my sins. It's hard for me to understand how You could possibly love me when I do so many things on a daily basis that must hurt You.

And yet You pardon my sins. You do not stay angry at me or hold grudges. You cast my sins into the depths of the ocean where they could never possibly be found again. You walk all over them, crushing all my sins into unrecognizable pieces.

You do this because You delight in unchanging love. Your love for me will not change when I change or when circumstances change. You won't grow weary of loving me or decide that it would be easier to stop loving me. Your love is not fickle or based on what I have done. You don't love me out of duty; instead, You *delight* in loving me.

Thank You for the immense confidence and peace I have knowing that I don't have to work for Your love or be afraid that I will lose it. Amen.

His Helping Hand

"So do not fear, for I am with you; do not be dismayed,
for I am your God. I will strengthen you and help you;
I will uphold you with my righteous right hand."
ISAIAH 41:10 NIV

Heavenly Father, Your Word promises me Your hand will never be too short to save me. Those times when I feel alone and lost, You are there. You have loved me with an everlasting love, and nothing can separate me from You. When I call, You will answer. When I fall, You will lift me up. When I repent, You are faithful and just to forgive me. On those days when hurt overcomes my heart, You comfort me and bring healing. You shine Your light into my heart to dispel any darkness.

Today I refuse to fear. I put my hope and trust in You. No matter what the day brings, You continually offer Your help. I want to be self-sufficient, but I understand You created me to depend on You. Sometimes it is difficult for me to ask for help, but I ask for Your help today and accept it. I choose to live my life according to the purpose You have put in me. When I doubt or feel dismayed, remind me of Your presence; infuse me with Your strength. Pour hope, once again, upon me. I look to You. You are where my help comes from. Amen.

Art of Recollection

Oh give thanks to the LORD; call upon his name; make known his deeds among the peoples! Sing to him, sing praises to him; tell of all his wondrous works! Glory in his holy name; let the hearts of those who seek the LORD rejoice! Seek the LORD and his strength; seek his presence continually!
PSALM 105:1–4 ESV

Adonai, I give thanks to You before Your throne. I call on Your name, the name that is above every name, the only name in which I can find true and awesome worth. In the midst of my restless state, the Holy Spirit reminds me of Your always faithful outstretched arm. The arm that brought Your people out of Egypt, that returned the exiles from Babylon, that inflicted judgment in order to turn the hearts of Your children back to You, and that took on flesh to rescue humanity from its brokenness. I must recall Your actions so that I may be continually compelled to sing Your praises and to tell everyone I meet that You are wondrous. I seek You, Adonai, with every fiber of my being, and in my journey I receive joy. I desire Your strength, and You instill it in me. When I look for Your presence, You appear. Oh, but Abba, You have always been here. I need to look for You more—both in Your past and present actions. Help me seek You continually. In doing so, I remember, I thank, I glory, and I rejoice in You. Amen.

A Restful Heart

"Come to Me, all who are weary and heavy-laden,
and I will give you rest."
MATTHEW 11:28 NASB

*H*elp me, Lord Jesus, for grief weighs down my heart. Turmoil surrounds me. I hit a brick wall no matter where I turn. My life is shrouded in darkness. I see no light in this bleak tunnel of misery. This burden is too heavy for me to bear alone. Yet is it as heavy as the crossbeam You had to carry after being whipped and tortured?

In His unfailing compassion, the heavenly Father graciously helped You in that dark hour. Simon of Cyrene carried the cross to Golgotha for You. Will God offer the same assistance for me?

Ah yes, but He has.

In Your suffering, You left an example for me to follow. As You gave up the burden of the crossbeam to Simon, I must give up my burden to You. For by Your wounds I am healed of my sorrow. I can take Your yoke upon me and learn from You. You teach me to lean on You in such a time as this. Oh, my Savior, take this weight from my shoulders and don't let me take it back.

In Your humble and gentle heart, You offer relief for my weary soul. As I surrender my trouble to You, my heart can rest in the comfort of Your tenderness.

Thank You, gracious Lord, for carrying my cross for me. Amen.

Beautiful in His Sight

My darling, you are lovely, so very lovely—as you look
through your veil, your eyes are those of a dove. Your hair
tosses about as gracefully as goats coming down from Gilead.
SONG OF SOLOMON 4:1 CEV

Lord, I spend a lot of time trying to look my best, but still I don't always like what I see in the mirror. Sometimes I am unhappy with the way that I look, and I worry that others might judge me. I feel anxious when my hair isn't styled just right or when my clothing doesn't fit as well as it could. There are some days when I think I'm just a mess.

Too often I forget that You made me, and You made me beautiful. In Your eyes, there are no bad hair days or fat days. There's just me.

My purpose is to honor You, Lord, in all that I do. The latest fashions, makeup, hairstyles—none of that matters to You. It is my heart that You see. It is the beautiful soul that You made me to be.

So, on those days when my clothes feel tight, or when I don't have the time or energy to fix myself up, put on makeup, and do my hair, remind me that I'm still beautiful. Stop me from worrying about how others perceive me. Allow me to see myself through Your eyes and always to like what I see. Amen.

Intangible Hope

But we are not of those who shrink back and are destroyed, but of those who have faith and preserve their souls. . . . Now faith is the assurance of things hoped for, the conviction of things not seen. For by it the people of old received their commendation. By faith we understand that the universe was created by the word of God, so that what is seen was not made out of things that are visible.
HEBREWS 10:39; 11:1–3 ESV

Father, I confess that I do shrink back and turn to the sins that destroy me and my trust in You. I confess that I desire to please others more than You, and most of my kind acts are performed for manipulation rather than Your glory. Father, I place my frayed and worried heart on the altar for You. To me it seems a pitiful offer, but to You it is the heart of Your redeemed and beloved child.

Father, grant me courage to rest in the unknown, the courage to trust in Your undisclosed will, and the strength to obey when nothing appears clear. Though it seems backward to the world, thank You that I do not know the future, because in not knowing I rely on You. Father, help me call on You and not revert to my destructive and manipulative tendencies. You have control of the visible and invisible world; help me remain steadfast in the knowledge of Your presence, grace, righteousness, and omnipotence.

He Cares

Give all your worries and cares to God, for he cares about you.
1 PETER 5:7 NLT

*D*ear Father, can I be honest with You? I love this verse, this reminder that You care deeply about me. But sometimes, Father, it doesn't feel that way. Sometimes it seems like You've forgotten me.

I have to remind myself often that feelings are different from facts. My feelings can be swayed by my health, my hormones, even by an unkind word or action. When I'm not feeling well or someone has hurt my feelings, it can appear that no one cares. And that includes You.

But facts are different. Facts can't be argued with. And because I know all Your words are true, I can be certain You care about me. I also know that You love me more than Your own life, You have good plans for me, and You will never, ever leave me. I'm confident that when I delight in You, when I think of You and trust You completely, You will give me the desires of my heart.

Help me trust in Your timing, Lord. Just because I don't see the answers to my prayers right now doesn't mean those answers aren't coming. And just because things aren't going well for me doesn't mean You don't care. I know You care, I know You love me, and I know You are bringing things together in my life for a good purpose.

I trust in You and Your care for me. Amen.

God Loves Us Unconditionally

The LORD did not set his love upon you, nor choose you, because ye were more in number than any people; for ye were the fewest of all people: but because the LORD loved you, and because he would keep the oath which he had sworn unto your fathers, hath the LORD brought you out with a mighty hand, and redeemed you out of the house of bondmen, from the hand of Pharaoh king of Egypt.

DEUTERONOMY 7:7–8 KJV

Lord, I'm so glad You don't choose only certain people to love. If You did, I might not make the cut—me and many others like me. I'm not one of the rich, beautiful, or famous, yet You loved me enough to send Your Son to die in my place. You loved the Israelites in spite of the fact that they were slaves in Egypt. You loved the apostle Paul despite the fact that he tortured and sentenced to death many Christians before he met You.

Verses 7 and 8 of Deuteronomy 7 tell me You didn't choose the Israelites because they were a great nation; they were the fewest of all peoples. You delivered them because You loved them.

Help me realize the greatness of Your unconditional love toward me. Without Your love, I would be nothing. I worship You because You loved me when I was unlovable and drew me in to become a part of Your family.

Father, help me show others Your unconditional love. Amen.

Strength and Shield

The LORD is my strength and my shield;
my heart trusts in him, and he helps me.
PSALM 28:7 NIV

*D*ear Father, sometimes it's easier to trust You with the big stuff. I trust that I can drive to the grocery store safely; I know You'll protect me, and if I die, I'll spend eternity with You. I trust that I won't get struck by lightning. I even trust You to take care of my need for food and clothing. But, Father, often the things that make me anxious and tear my heart to pieces aren't *things* at all; they're people.

I worry that my teenage daughter will always loathe me. I worry that my son won't make good choices. I worry that people will say and do things to hurt me. Relationships, Father. . .those are what bring me the most anxiety.

But You are my strength, Father, in every situation. You make me emotionally strong so I can handle unkind remarks and hurtful actions with grace and love. You are my shield, which means even when hard things come You'll protect me so they don't destroy me. I know that in every situation You will help me. I trust You, Lord. When I start to worry about things that haven't happened, remind me of Your goodness. When I feel anxious about my relationships, help me trust in You, trust Your timing, and cling to the strength and shield You promised to provide. Amen.

Hope

Not only that, but we rejoice in our sufferings, knowing that suffering produces
endurance, and endurance produces character, and character produces hope,
and hope does not put us to shame, because God's love has been poured into
our hearts through the Holy Spirit who has been given to us.
ROMANS 5:3–5 ESV

*F*ather, there are times when my only hope is in Your sovereignty. You do not take away the pain, but You give me hope, and hope does not put me to shame. I should not listen to the lies that preach there is no way out, no resolution. In Lamentations 3:25 (NIV), You say, "The LORD is good to those whose hope is in him." You are good, because You are unchanging. Nothing affects You, though everything is affected by You.

I cannot settle on simple truths that I store in the back of my mind and over time become myth. I must dwell and hope in the true truths of Your character: You are love, You are infinite, You are all-powerful, You are compassionate, and You are just. These are a few of Your attributes. As quoted in Job, "Though he slay me, I will hope in him" (13:15 ESV). I trust that You will fulfill Your promise of goodness. May I hold fast to the testimony and beauty of Jesus Christ!

Lord, I confess this prideful sin that I see myself as superior. Forgive me and break me of this judgmental heart. You have blessed me with the opportunity to reach out and connect with those who are hurting, but I need Your courage and strength to act. Help me submit and walk with You through these hard times. Amen.

Worry vs. Faith

"Therefore I tell you, do not worry about your life, what you
will eat or drink; or about your body, what you will wear.
Is not life more than food, and the body more than clothes?"
MATTHEW 6:25 NIV

Lord, it's so easy to give You my concerns and then act as if they are still mine. Even though I know I'm helpless to change anything and the most powerful thing I can possibly do is pray, still I worry. Thank You, Lord, for showing me over and over how eager You are to care for me. Please forgive me for doubting—or for thinking You wouldn't be interested.

I know You are able, so when I doubt, it's really Your love I question. And yet You continue to pour out Your goodness on me. I surely disappoint You with my lack of faith, but You don't give up on me.

The Bible says that You give us a measure of faith (Romans 12:3). I am sure Your measure is never stingy, so I ask You to make me ready to accept all You have for me. If I fill my life with worry, there's no room for the faith You yearn to give. I want to be as eager to receive Your good gifts as You are to give them. I hold out my empty vessel and ask You to fill me to overflowing with Your faith, to believe You have everything under control. You are magnificent! Amen.

Christ Has Overcome

*"These things I have spoken to you, so that in Me you
may have peace. In the world you have tribulation,
but take courage; I have overcome the world."*
JOHN 16:33 NASB

*L*ord, forgive me when I seek to find peace in anything else other than You. It is only in You that I can have true, lasting peace. But You do not offer a peace that promises a complete voidance of any trials or difficulties. In fact, in this verse You tell me that I *will* have tribulation. This world will inevitably contain heartbreak, hurt, regret, anxiety, and difficulties.

But You have overcome the world.

What an incredible truth! I need not worry when I face seemingly insurmountable struggles, because You have already fought the battle and You have conquered. I can come to You with my heartbreaks and my worry, confident that they are no match for You. No circumstance and no enemy on this earth is too mighty for You. You have already overcome all that this world can throw at me.

This is true peace—to have complete confidence that You are the victorious Ruler of this world. May I take courage in this and live my life in light of Your victory. I bring all the things that have been causing me anxiety and sadness before You now and lay them at the feet of the King. Amen.

All of You

Trust in the LORD with all your heart, and do not lean on your own understanding. In all your ways acknowledge him, and he will make straight your paths.
PROVERBS 3:5–6 ESV

Lord, You will never fail me. Why do I think I can resolve things myself? Why do I put my hope in people? Why do I look to them for wisdom and understanding? Forgive me. You have all the answers I need. You are the wisdom I seek and the understanding I desire. You have a purpose and a plan—for my day, for my year, for my life.

You are all I need. You have set a course before me and given me the map. The direction I need for my life and my future rest in study of Your holy Word, time with You in prayer, and a decision to follow Your peace in my heart. My heart will never be deceived as long as I follow You. I refuse to become lost in my own plans—or making things go my own way. Give me Your perspective. Bring me up to a higher place so that I have a more complete picture of You and where You are taking me. I acknowledge You today and will testify to the truth that all I am, and all I have, You've made possible by Your grace. It's not because of anything I've done but because of everything You've done. Amen.

Fear-Fighting Love

There is no fear in love, but perfect love casts out fear.
For fear has to do with punishment, and whoever fears has
not been perfected in love. We love because he first loved us.
1 JOHN 4:18–19 ESV

All-abounding Love, this unsettling spirit that burdens me rises not from a concerned heart but from fear. Fear that I may leave something undone, fear that I am inadequate, fear that I will disappoint You. Thank You for revealing this to me. Now I know the next step is to break me of it. Guide me through situations in which I clearly see Your love shatter man-made barriers and overcome injustices. Let me love and serve boldly not by my own power and not to achieve my own limited vision. Spur me on by the everlasting Love, who is perfect—in mind, will, and action—and who infuses the faithful with Your strength. Wipe clean my heart of guilt and purge me of my fear. I ask that the intensely beautiful and inimitably Good News of Jesus would draw me to a deeper understanding of Your grace. That I may walk not in the fear of punishment but in the joy of this life-giving mercy. Point me every day to the price Christ paid. Perfect me so that I may reflect the image of my Father and fight the fears in my heart, and in the hearts of others, with Your love. Amen.

A Protected Heart

In peace I will both lie down and sleep, for You alone,
O Lord, make me to dwell in safety.
PSALM 4:8 NASB

Dear God, when I lie in bed at night, my spinning thoughts keep me awake. The issues of my day tick off the to-do list, one by one. Did I complete all my tasks? Did I forget anything or anyone in the rush of business?

A noise outside startles me, turning my thoughts to danger. Are the doors and windows locked? No need to fear. It's merely a gentle wind blowing through the trees.

Sirens blare in the distance. Fire trucks? Are the batteries in my smoke alarm up-to-date? Or does one of those sirens belong to an ambulance? Has a friend or family member had an accident or become deathly ill?

Lord, these worries don't come from You but from the enemy. You hold my days and nights in Your capable hands. For I know You are faithful and will strengthen and protect me from the evil one (2 Thessalonians 3:3).

In You I have all the protection I need against these fretful barbs hurled at me. Help me focus on You instead of the disturbances around me. Only then will I "both lie down and sleep, for You alone, O Lord, make me to dwell in safety."

Thank You, faithful Lord, for comforting my anxious heart with the security of Your protection.

In Jesus' name I pray. Amen.

When Waiting Is Hard

But they soon forgot what he had done
and did not wait for his plan to unfold.
PSALM 106:13 NIV

Lord, by faith I know that, no matter what lies ahead of me, You are already there. You have gone ahead to prepare for my arrival. But I am like a little child. I want to know what You have planned for me. I want to tear off the wrapping paper and see what's inside.

"*Wait,*" You tell me. "*It's not time.*"

But, Lord, I want to know. I want to know right now. Impatience is my enemy. When I pray and ask You for something, I expect You to answer my prayer right away. When You don't, I become anxious and discouraged. I question You: "Why won't You give me what I've asked for? Why do You make me wait?"

I'm pitiful at waiting, and I need Your help with that. Please teach me to wait patiently for You. I know that patience equals peace, and oh, how blessed it would be to wait peacefully for You to act. Lord, help me keep my thoughts fixed on Your goodness and all that You have done for me. Fill up my heart with hope. Give me an attitude of joyful anticipation. Strengthen my faith in Your timing. You have never let me down, and I know that You will answer my prayer—maybe not now, but exactly when the time is right. Amen.

How Fickle

And he is the head of the body, the church.
He is the beginning, the firstborn from the dead,
that in everything he might be preeminent.
COLOSSIANS 1:18 ESV

*F*ather, do I live in the deeply rooted knowledge that You control everything? In this verse are a few of Your true characteristics, the very fibers of Your being: You are the beginning, the conqueror of death, You exist in everything, and nothing is outside of You. I place my hope and trust in all manner of fickle things such as medicine, science, money, and myself.

Lord, there is nothing on this earth that protects me but You. If You reign over all things and have set a course for my life, then You are my sole protector and protector of my soul. Lord, help me turn to You with the "little" things: What present should I give a friend or loved one? Should I volunteer for that event? Is it right to stay late and get ahead of my work? All these decisions I take into my own hands because they seem so insignificant, yet You purchased my life with Yours; therefore, nothing is insignificant to You.

Father, reveal to me the fickle things that I place trust in and help me turn to You with my "little" prayers and questions. When storms arise, the little moments and short trials secure my trust in You. Thank You that You are steadfast. Thank You that You are not fickle and You cannot deny Your holiness and justice, or compassion. Amen.

Complete Trust

I sought the LORD, and he answered me;
he delivered me from all my fears.
PSALM 34:4 NIV

*D*ear Father, I have prayed, but I still feel anxious and afraid. I'm waiting for You to answer me, and while I wait, I worry.

I suppose there's a lesson there. I know that while You care about my circumstances, You care more about my soul. When You don't answer right away, the way I want You to answer, You're trying to teach me something. In this case, I think You might be teaching me to trust You.

In order to truly trust, I have to calm down. I have to believe in my heart that You are working everything out in a beautiful way, to an end so much better than I could think up in my human mind. When I try to write my own problem-solving plan of attack and then issue You orders to carry out that plan, I limit my options.

Help me bring You my problems, but not my solutions. Help me to truly cast my cares on You and then leave You to solve them while I live calmly and with serenity. I know anxiety is the opposite of trust, so help me, Lord. Help me trust You. I know when I truly believe You are actively working to care for me and my problems, my fear dissipates. It isn't through rote prayers but through total and complete trust that I become free. Amen.

Rest in the Lord

*Rest in the LORD, and wait patiently for him: fret
not thyself because of him who prospereth in his way,
because of the man who bringeth wicked devices to pass.*
PSALM 37:7 KJV

Lord, forgive me when I am fretful about what others are doing, what they're accomplishing in life and their seeming prosperity. Help me not to point at them and say, "They're prospering in spite of their wickedness." I confess it's sometimes hard to ignore the fact that I'm working much harder than they are and they seem to be the one getting ahead.

Show me how to stop fretting and rest in You, Lord. Turn my eyes away from the world and its definition of success. Help me focus on You. Allow me to see what You want me to accomplish and what You want me to be for Your glory, not mine. Help me rest in You until I find my place in Your will.

Waiting patiently for You while I'm learning to rest is a hard thing to do. It means I must go through frustration and trouble to get to that place. But in order to be what You want me to be, teach me how to wait patiently. I know You will see me through.

Forgive me, Lord, for focusing on the ones who, in the end, bring wicked devices to pass. They aren't my example. You are. Amen.

You'll Always Be the Same

There should be a consistency that runs through us all.
For Jesus doesn't change—yesterday, today,
tomorrow, he's always totally himself.
HEBREWS 13:7–8 MSG

Thank You, Lord Jesus, that even though circumstances change and my own heart is often fickle, You are always the same. Your endless, unconditional love for me never changes. That's incredible! I don't even like myself sometimes, but You forgive my foolish attitudes, my selfishness, and all my faltering ways. Thank You, Lord.

You don't wait until I prove my allegiance or show that I can overcome temptations. Sometimes I'm so ashamed of the way I treat others, the things I say, and my lack of faith, but I don't have to accomplish great feats for You to love me. When I behave like a spoiled child, You love me. When I say ugly things, You love me. I can't comprehend such love; I can only praise You. You are amazing!

I give You every bit of myself, Lord, knowing that only as I totally depend on Your unchanging love and grace will I begin to be more like You. I open my life to You. Fill me to the brim with Your Holy Spirit so others can see Your consistent love in me.

I might change my behavior temporarily, but I can't remake myself. Only You can create a new heart in me that is stable and unchanging in the midst of life's issues. You're wonderful! Amen.

Do Not Fear

" 'Do not fear, for I am with you; do not anxiously look about
you, for I am your God. I will strengthen you, surely I will help
you, surely I will uphold you with My righteous right hand.' "
ISAIAH 41:10 NASB

Lord, I have no reason to fear, because You are with me. You are ever present by my side to guide and protect me. The things in this world that make me afraid are not more powerful than You and are not out of Your control.

I need not look anxiously around me for help from somewhere else, because You are my God. Keep me from setting up other things in my life as gods. Nothing and no one else besides You is able to give me the peace, endurance, and power I need to face the day ahead. Instead of looking around me and focusing on the things that overwhelm me, may I set my gaze firmly and unwaveringly on You.

Thank You for this wonderful reminder that You will strengthen and help me. I ask You, the almighty God, for that strength and help right now as I face the days and weeks ahead.

Help me rest securely in the knowledge that I am firmly placed in Your hands.

I truly have no reason to fear with You by my side, as my God, strengthening, helping, and holding me in Your hands. Amen.

Following the Spirit of God

For though we walk in the flesh, we are not waging war according to the flesh.
For the weapons of our warfare are not of the flesh but have divine power to
destroy strongholds. We destroy arguments and every lofty opinion raised against
the knowledge of God, and take every thought captive to obey Christ.
2 Corinthians 10:3–5 esv

Heavenly Father, You have created me in Your image to be spirit-led. Once I gave my heart to You, I was no longer ruled by my body but by my inner person. I am connected to You—spirit to Spirit. You lead me; You guide me, and I choose to follow Your ways. Living by my flesh is easy—it's a habit. Choosing to let my spirit direct me takes more effort, but it is the way I should go. It is the way I want to live for You. Forgive me when I fall into the habits of my old life, when my old nature becomes emotional and I demand my own way. I am a spirit; I live in a body. My body is created by You to follow my spirit's lead.

Help me remember: flesh feeds flesh and spirit feeds spirit. Lead me, guide me, and teach me! I can let myself go and respond emotionally to the circumstances around me, or I can choose Your way and respond by letting my spirit lead me into peace—Your peace. I set my heart and mind on You. I choose Your peace today. Amen.

Guided into Peace

So the church throughout all Judea and Galilee and Samaria
had peace and was being built up. And walking in the fear of
the Lord and in the comfort of the Holy Spirit, it multiplied.
ACTS 9:31 ESV

God of order, Your peace truly goes beyond the limits of my understanding. Luke recounts the persecution of believers, especially of Saul-turned-Paul, in the book of Acts, and then he writes that, as a result, the church had peace. Their lives were threatened, they were pursued on every side, and yet they had peace! How is this possible? Powerfully gentle Abba, You show us that it is faith in Your sovereignty that gave them peace and continues to calm anxious and frightened believers today. The only sane manner in which to deal with hostility and uncertainty is to let ourselves be guided by Your peace. Thank You that the figure of Your Son is the source and sustenance of this peace, which builds up Your children individually and Your church collectively. Like Jesus, help Your people walk in obedience to Your goodness and in the joy that You provide through the Comforter—the Holy Spirit. Mold meekness into Your children because, as You revealed to King David, it is the humble who will receive Your inheritance and who will "delight themselves in abundant peace" (Psalm 37:11 ESV). Then let praise burst from our lips as we see the family grow in number and in likeness to You. Amen.

A Contented Heart

"And who of you by being worried can add a single hour to his life?
And why are you worried about clothing? Observe how the lilies of the
field grow; they do not toil nor do they spin, yet I say to you that not
even Solomon in all his glory clothed himself like one of these."
MATTHEW 6:27–29 NASB

*D*ear Lord, I struggle with anxiety as my paycheck dwindles. Too many obligations outweigh my salary. I stretch it across the sea of my monthly living expenses of mortgage, utilities, and food costs. My clothes need to be repaired or replaced. The cupboard is nearly empty. My fourteen-year-old car needs new tires. Do I let worry shorten my life span? May it never be!

I smile when I see flowers blooming nearby, and remember You said not to worry about such things. You clothe flowers in beautiful, multicolored blossoms and nurture them. Surely You will meet my needs. You always do.

You didn't promise me immunity to trials. But You did promise to take care of me. Your provision can come through a helping hand from a friend or relative. You could surprise me with the benevolent gift from a stranger. On rare occasions, it's as miraculous as watering a garden with a raindrop.

In times of want and plenty, I say with the apostle Paul: "I have learned to be content in whatever circumstances I am" (Philippians 4:11 NASB).

Your provision in all circumstances, Father God, fills my heart with contentment. Amen.

Breathe

Let everything that has breath
praise the LORD. Praise the LORD.
PSALM 150:6 NIV

*D*ear heavenly Father, when anxiety grips me, tell me to breathe. Tell me to breathe in, full and slow. With every breath, allow me to draw You deep into my heart. Wash out all the worry there, and refresh me with Your endless love.

Father, at the moment I was born, You gave me the breath of life. Then You breathed into me all Your goodness and the potential to live my life worry-free. You gave me Your scriptures to teach and sustain me. And how many times have You breathed the Holy Spirit into my troubled soul to soothe me and make things right?

Now I need to remember and breathe. I need to remember to breathe You in and to allow You to calm me. With every breath I take I will praise You. I will keep in mind that You have control of my anxious heart and there is no room there for worry or fear.

Come now, Holy Spirit, and grant me Your peace. I breathe in Your presence. I breathe out the worry. I breathe in God's love. I breathe out the fear.

Oh, heavenly Father, You fill me up! You take my anxious thoughts away. I praise You for every deep, cleansing breath. I praise You for giving me life. I know that You will calm me down—if only I remember to breathe. Amen.

Keep Calm and Do Nothing

"The Lord will fight for you, and you have only to be silent."
Exodus 14:14 ESV

*I*n this day and age when action is so heavily stressed, it is hard for me to wrap my head around the thought of not acting. Lord, is this truly a command You give in times of struggle? Waiting on Your will and timing is one of the hardest tasks.

I must remember Your might and power. You created the very atoms of the ground I tread, and I confess that many times I stomp around creating chaos when all I seek is order. Lord, the thought of ceasing my plans and obeying Your will frightens me. I have an idea of the road You wish me to walk, and it is far outside my comfort zone. But then I think of the times I wrestled with Your plan, gave in, and rejoiced in Your work! When You call me to reach outside of myself and forgive or trust, it tears me from my selfish pride, rids me of embittered desires, and cleanses the channels of my heart. I must trust that the most strenuous and arduous tasks You grant me will bear the most fruit and draw me closer to You. To know that the God of the universe fights for me, an undeserving sinner, leaves me astounded.

Lord, thank You for fighting the battles inside my heart and outside of myself. Change my heart, Lord; help me obey Your command and trust in Your plan. Let Your Spirit prompt me to keep silent and listen for Your instruction. Lord, grant me the courage to release these fears into Your care and stand firm in the fact that You will fight for me. Amen.

Angel Warriors

The angel of the Lord encamps around
those who fear him, and he delivers them.
PSALM 34:7 NIV

*D*ear Father, it's comforting to know Your angels set up camp around me. I know they're protecting me. But they do even more than that. At Your bidding, they will deliver me from whatever trials may come.

When I feel discouraged, I know Your Holy Spirit encourages me. It helps to picture those angels cheering me on, as they surround me with their battle-ready suits of armor. "Go on! You can do it! Be strong and courageous!" I don't have to fight the world alone. And the thought of them "encamping" around me lets me know they came ready to stay. They're not planning to leave me.

I'm confident that, whatever I face, You will bring me through it. Your angels will fight to keep my body, my mind, and my emotions safe and strong. Though life certainly will bring some scars, I will not be destroyed. I can move forward, knowing I am safe and protected in Your care. I can face whatever comes, certain that when all is said and done I will stand victorious.

Thank You for this reminder that I am never alone. I have Your Holy Spirit helping me along and Your angels watching over me. When I feel discouraged or afraid today, remind me of that picture of Your angels surrounding and protecting me. Amen.

The Throne of Grace

*Let us therefore come boldly unto the throne of grace, that we
may obtain mercy, and find grace to help in time of need.*
HEBREWS 4:16 KJV

*L*ord, why is it so hard to let go of problems and turn them over to You? I know the best place for them is in Your capable hands. I carry problems around and worry over them when all I need to do is approach the throne. You're there, ready and waiting, to take the weight off my shoulders and give me rest from my burdens.

Lord, give me boldness through the Holy Spirit to approach You. Help me not to feel like I'm trespassing. Your sacrifice on the cross has made it possible to enter into the Holy of Holies and talk to You personally. No need for anyone else to be present.

Lord, I accept the mercy You so willingly offer. Help me show that mercy to others just as You have shown it to me.

Sometimes life gets wearisome and I'd like to stop and rest, but there's no time. Lord, help me pursue the grace to make it through the hard times and finish the journey. Lord, help me extend grace to others, even those I feel don't deserve it. I didn't deserve grace either, but You supplied a generous portion just for me.

Thank You, Lord, for the gifts of boldness, grace, and mercy and the privilege to come to You. Amen.

Christ's Power in Me

But he said to me, "My grace is sufficient for you, for my power is made perfect in weakness." Therefore I will boast all the more gladly about my weaknesses, so that Christ's power may rest on me.

2 CORINTHIANS 12:9 NIV

I want to be strong and able—to conquer all my fears and win every battle—but the truth is that I'm only victorious when I depend on You, Lord. Your grace is always enough. You tell me to love others, even my enemies. You tell me to forgive those who treat me wrong or hurt someone I love. I can't do that on my own. Thank You for.grace that perfects my weakness.

The idea of Your power resting on me is awesome, Jesus. I long to understand that truth, but first, I know I have to stop depending on my own strength. Can I boast in my own weaknesses? Only when I realize I can't manage this life without Your grace.

Little by little, I realize what freedom I can enjoy when I stop trying to make it on my own. Sometimes I can't even keep myself from thinking I have to earn Your grace or that I deserve it because of my actions. You've given me so much, Lord, but nothing is really mine. As I learn to be a good steward of the gifts You give, I understand more about how precious Your grace is. Thank You! Amen.

God Is for Us

What then shall we say to these things? If God is for us,
who is against us? He who did not spare His own Son,
but delivered Him over for us all, how will He not
also with Him freely give us all things?
ROMANS 8:31–32 NASB

Lord, what an amazing thought this is that You, the Creator and Sustainer of the universe, are *for me*. Who can possibly do anything against me with You on my side? Nothing can happen to me that is outside of Your will. Even the most difficult and heartbreaking experiences You will redeem and use for my good and Your glory because You are *for me*.

Lord, You loved me enough that You gave the life of Your Son in exchange for my life. I cannot comprehend this kind of love. I do not deserve it. I am not nearly grateful enough for it. But nevertheless, You continue to lavish it on me. In light of this immense and unwarranted love, may I be confident to bring You any and all of my concerns and desires. If You love me this much, then You certainly want me to come to You and have a close relationship with You.

Since You loved me enough to give Your Son for me, I can be confident that nothing You do will be to my detriment. Even when I don't understand how my circumstances could possibly be for my good or Your glory, grant me the faith I need to persevere and trust You. Amen.

Help My Unbelief

"'If you can'?" said Jesus. "Everything is possible for one
who believes." Immediately the boy's father exclaimed,
"I do believe; help me overcome my unbelief!"
MARK 9:23–24 NIV

Lord, I believe in You, and I know You are real. Even though I can't see You, I experience Your presence and know You are with me. Thank You for the measure of faith You have given me. Thank You for the many wonderful things You've done in my life. Thank You for saving me from everything I need to be saved from on a daily basis.

I know You can do miracles. The fact that I am on this earth and living for You is a miracle. Sometimes I get lost in my own mind, trying to figure out how You're going to turn things around—how You're going to answer my prayer and deliver on Your promise. I am so limited on what I understand, but as I spend time with You in prayer and study Your Word, my knowledge and understanding will increase.

You said everything is possible—only believe! So I believe; I want to believe. When I doubt or try to reason it all out in my mind, help my unbelief. You can, and it's not for me to figure it out. Forgive me and help me trust You. I leave the challenges I'm facing right now in Your faithful hands. Amen.

A Prayer to the God of My Life

Why are you cast down, O my soul, and why are you in turmoil within me?
Hope in God; for I shall again praise him, my salvation and my God.
My soul is cast down within me; therefore I remember you from the
land of Jordan and of Hermon, from Mount Mizar.
PSALM 42:5–6 ESV

Horn of my salvation, I cling to You for strength. I cry out in frustration, like the sons of Korah who wrote Psalm 42: "Why, my soul, are you downcast?" (NIV). God has not been unseated from His heavenly throne. Why do I let such turmoil grow inside me? God is no less powerful than when He drew His children out of slavery in Egypt, provided angel armies to fight alongside His people, or conquered sin to provide a way of rescue for creation. Yet there are those who chide, "Where is your God?" My soul thirsts for You, the living God, but my tears have been my food. From the depths of sadness I call to You. My hope is in You alone. Hear my supplication. I praise You that You hear and that Your grace heals. In the words of Martin Luther, "I put my trust in You, Lord, and not in my own merit. On You my soul shall rest; Your word upholds my fainting spirit. Your promised mercy is my fort, my comfort, and my sweet support." Good Shepherd, Your people look to the hope of final freedom from sin and sorrow. Amen.

A Trusting Heart

In God I have put my trust, I shall not be afraid.
What can man do to me?
PSALM 56:11 NASB

*F*ather God, *I trust you* are three of the most encouraging—and yet frightening—words we can say to one another. When we trust others to manage our circumstances, we give them control and pray they make the right choices. A wrong decision could bring disastrous results. On the other hand, we carry that burden for our loved ones when they put their trust in us, plus the weight of any mistakes we make.

How blessed I am that I can put my trust in You, Lord! I am confident in the fact that You don't make mistakes. You know my past, present, and future, as well as every hair on my head. I can completely let go of the situation and rely on You. "For You have delivered my soul from death, indeed my feet from stumbling, so that I may walk before God in the light of the living" (Psalm 56:13 NASB).

Trusting in You, Father, means to have faith in You, to depend on You, and best of all, to let go of my worries. You have freed me from spiritual death. Walking before You in the light of the living means sharing eternal life. I will not stumble when I trust in You.

Thank You, dear God, for trusting me to trust in You. Amen.

Opposites Attract

The Spirit and your desires are enemies of each other.
They are always fighting each other and keeping
you from doing what you feel you should.
GALATIANS 5:17 CEV

*D*ear God, sometimes I feel like there is a tug-of-war going on inside me. I am pulled this way and that way, toward You and away from You. I hate that feeling. It leaves me restless and scattered. But I know that there is a way out of this limbo. It comes from reading scripture and also from being aware of Your presence in my life.

There is a saying that opposites attract, and I am beginning to see that it's true. You are teaching me that every negative thought and feeling attracts me to a deeper relationship with You. I am learning to see Your goodness in everything. When Satan knocks me down, You lift me up. When I feel weak, You give me strength. You turn darkness into light, and my despair turns to hope whenever I put my faith in You. Even in tragedies and disasters I see Your goodness. You heal the sick and the injured. You comfort the ones who mourn. When evil tears something down, You build it up better than before.

Oh, God, You are so good! Keep on teaching me that opposites attract. Continue to show me Your grace and Your goodness, and whenever I feel myself tugged away, pull me nearer to You. Amen.

My God

He will swallow up death forever; and the Lord GOD will wipe away tears from all faces, and the reproach of his people he will take away from all the earth, for the LORD has spoken. It will be said on that day, "Behold, this is our God; we have waited for him, that he might save us. This is the LORD; we have waited for him; let us be glad and rejoice in his salvation."

ISAIAH 25:8–9 ESV

*L*ord, You have written the earth's story and have given Your children the manuscript. We were not created for death; You said Yourself that You have set eternity in our hearts. These days the world sets a price on my soul. I feel a debt measure up against my time and energy, and I find myself defaulting, unable to devote any more of myself. But You do not rely on time; time relies on You, and the same grace and mercy You showed the Israelites is the same grace and mercy You bestow on me.

I wait for You in storms, calm, calamity, and confusion; I wait for Your return. You are my God. You are the God who cannot be shaken, and though people try to deny You, they are wishful thinkers. No science can equate Your power; we can only glimpse what You desire to demonstrate. And yet next to Your might is a God who wipes away my tears and purges the world of suffering. You are my God. Amen.

Fear and Hope

"Therefore do not worry about tomorrow, for tomorrow will worry about itself. Each day has enough trouble of its own."
MATTHEW 6:34 NIV

*D*ear Father, it's so hard not to worry about the future! Sometimes I let my mind wander, and I concoct all sorts of awful scenarios in my mind. What will happen to me when I'm old? Will I have enough money to live on? What will happen to my children? Will they be safe? What if some terrible disease afflicts me or someone I love? But You said I'm not supposed to worry about the future. You want me to take one day at a time and deal with the things that are right in front of me.

I am learning the difference between fear and hope. Fear is the belief that something bad is going to happen; hope is the belief that something good is going to happen. When I worry, I demonstrate a belief that bad things will come.

I don't believe this verse is telling me not to plan for the future. Rather, I think You want me to plan with wisdom and hope, believing in Your goodness. You don't want me to worry, because worry indicates fear.

Help me plan wisely, with a joyful belief that Your goodness and blessings await. Remind me of Your love, and fill my heart with excitement over all the beautiful experiences You have planned. Amen.

Conquering Fear

But the LORD said to me, "Do not say, 'I am too young.'
You must go to everyone I send you to and say whatever
I command you. Do not be afraid of them, for I am with
you and will rescue you," declares the LORD. Then the
LORD reached out his hand and touched my mouth and
said to me, "I have put my words in your mouth."
JEREMIAH 1:7–9 NIV

I confess, Lord, sometimes I'm afraid to say and do the things You ask of me. I don't know if it's the task or what people will think. Maybe it's a little of both. Just when I think I've got this fear conquered, it rears its ugly head again.

I pray for the courage to stand and speak when You require it of me. Your Word declares that You will give me the words I need. I must trust You for those words. Help me not to worry whether I am qualified to speak or that others may consider me unqualified. You are the One who calls and qualifies the vessel You want to use for service. May I always be available to speak for You.

Give me strength to do the job You are calling me to do. Help me commit to getting the job done and doing it well for Your glory. When I feel afraid, help me remember that You are with me to rescue me from fear. Amen.

He Loves Me!

*And I am convinced that nothing can ever separate us from God's love.
Neither death nor life, neither angels nor demons, neither our fears for
today nor our worries about tomorrow—not even the powers of hell can
separate us from God's love. No power in the sky above or in the earth
below—indeed, nothing in all creation will ever be able to separate us
from the love of God that is revealed in Christ Jesus our Lord.*
ROMANS 8:38–39 NLT

Lord, these verses cover every obstacle my imagination can come up with, thinking You won't love me. The enemy tells me I have to be good enough to earn Your love, but that is such a lie. He tries to convince me that I'll never measure up and that I can't expect You to love someone like me. I've failed more often than I can remember. I've missed so many opportunities to tell others what You've done for me; I might as well deny I even know You. I judge others or treat them like they aren't worthy. I want people to see You in me, but my failures get in their way. Thank You, Lord, for loving me anyway.

You don't love me because of what I've done. You love me because of who You are. And You've proven that love by giving Your life to save me. Help me always to feel assured of Your love so I can pour it out to others. Amen.

No Separation

For I am convinced that neither death, nor life, nor angels,
nor principalities, nor things present, nor things to come, nor powers,
nor height, nor depth, nor any other created thing, will be able to
separate us from the love of God, which is in Christ Jesus our Lord.
ROMANS 8:38–39 NASB

Thank You, Lord. Thank You that absolutely nothing can separate me from Your love. Thank You that I do not need to be concerned or fear that somehow I won't be good enough to keep Your love. Thank You that I am forever, inextricably covered in Your love.

Not even death, which separates me from everything that I know here on earth, can cut me off from Your love. The things that happen in this life cannot separate me from You. No angel or any power is strong enough to break Your love for me.

None of the things that are hurting and breaking me now are able to separate me from Your love. Please show me Your love clearly and remind me that my circumstances are smaller and weaker than Your love.

There is nothing that can possibly happen in the future that will separate me from Your love. When the days and years ahead seem so uncertain and dark, one thing is for sure—You will still love me, no matter what.

Thank You that I have eternity to spend lavished in Your love. Amen.

Winning the Mind Games

Worry weighs a person down;
an encouraging word cheers a person up.
PROVERBS 12:25 NLT

Lord, I am learning worry can take over my mind, if I let it. You know exactly how many hours I've sat wide awake at night imagining different outcomes of different situations, worrying about what might or might not transpire as a result of my words, actions, or the consequences I find myself in. While it's good to think things through, I know You don't want me to have anxiety over how things turn out. Instead of thinking and rethinking how things might turn out or what I can do to resolve an issue, help me rest in Your peace.

I choose today to relax and settle my heart and mind. I focus my thoughts on You—on Your goodness, Your mercy, and Your love. You love me so much. You've promised to work all things together for my good because I love You. I push the negative thoughts out of my mind. I choose to fill my thoughts with Your Word and what it says about my life.

I am a child of the Most High, bought with a price, and I belong to You. I am free from condemnation. Nothing can separate me from Your love. You have not given me a spirit of fear but of power, love, and a sound mind. You have promised me peace, sweet peace. Thank You for that peace now. Amen.

Sustained Refuge

The salvation of the righteous is from the LORD; he is their stronghold in the time of trouble. The LORD helps them and delivers them; he delivers them from the wicked and saves them, because they take refuge in him.
PSALM 37:39–40 ESV

My strong Tower, help Your children to look for refuge only in You. Enlighten our minds and hearts to the specifics of what this means. How may Your people take refuge in You? We can only do so by recognizing You as King and by accepting Your offer of redemption as the only way of escaping the brokenness and rebellion of this world. We proclaim that You alone provide that rescue, and we bring You praise. Lead us to run daily to Your Word for guidance. This is the sword of the faithful, of those called righteous by the sacrifice of Jesus! Guide us to know and use this sword of the Spirit so that we may yield it powerfully and lovingly from within our tower of refuge, which is Christ. Forgive us when we treat slightingly communion with You through prayer. Remind Your people hourly that this fellowship is vital in considering You our place of safety. Let our words be the treasured incense that we bring to You, our Refuge. When troubles come, embolden us to trust singularly in You and in Your power for deliverance. You relieve anxious hearts when they lay all at Your feet. We thank You, Lord. You do not forsake Your saints. Amen.

A Stilled Heart

Be still, and know that I am God.
PSALM 46:10 KJV

Only You can still my restless heart, Lord. As the storm winds of stress toss me about like a boat without a rudder, I frantically reach out for a stable mast.

Is this what the disciples felt when the fierce gale blew the waves over their boat? Like them, I fear I'll sink in the storm. And like them, I must acknowledge Your greatness. You rescued them when You "arose, and rebuked the wind, and said unto the sea, Peace, be still. And the wind ceased, and there was a great calm" (Mark 4:39 KJV).

Help me to stop striving when storms come into my life. I realize I create my own hurricane-force winds and crashing waves when I fail to turn to You. Let me be as calm as the wind and sea were by Your command. For You are the one who stills "the noise of the seas, the noise of their waves, and the tumult of the people" (Psalm 65:7 KJV). If the wind and the sea obey You, then certainly the elements around me must do likewise.

And so must I.

When I remember to turn to You first and not when I've exhausted all other resources, the hectic episodes lose their strength. I have no storm to ride out in fear. For You are my refuge and my strength. I will be still and know that You are God. Amen.

Rejoice and Be Glad

This is the day which the Lᴏʀᴅ hath made;
we will rejoice and be glad in it.
Psalm 118:24 ᴋᴊᴠ

*D*ear Lord, I don't do very well on dark, stormy days. When gray clouds hide Your sapphire sky, a veil shrouds my heart—if I let it. But, Lord, I will fight it with all that I've got, because You made this day. You made this day, and I will be glad in it.

The day might look dreary, but still it overflows with Your goodness. Oh, Lord, You are so good! You woke me this morning, and You said to me, *"Child, I love you."* That alone brings sunshine into my heart. You give me shelter from the rain and warmth when it is cold. You meet my every need, and that, dear Lord, is cause to rejoice.

You open my senses to the beauty around me: the rhythm of the steady rain, the wind's song, the majestic sight of ragged clouds racing across a stormy sky. The lightning and thunder embody Your greatness. They reflect Your authority over heaven and earth. Rejoice and be glad! Rejoice! God is good!

Yes, Lord, You made this day, and just like every day, it is filled with the wonder of You. So I will not let a veil shroud my heart. I will not let gray skies bring me down. Instead, I will reflect on the goodness of You. I will reflect and be grateful and glad. Amen.

Overcome

This world overwhelms my heart, but You have overcome the world through Your perfect will and omnipotence, Lord. I am a child of the One who rules this world and has defeated all my fears. It is a humbling and reassuring promise that You instruct life's every turn and hear my cry. I thank You for being honest about the trials and providing Yourself as the Redeemer and remedy to all that bears me down.

Lord, there are so many times I have wanted to throw in the proverbial towel and give up the Christian walk, but out of Your grace and love, You won't give up on me. Thank You.

I praise You for not forsaking me. Forgive me for losing heart in You. Lord, may I remember Your perseverance when I am tempted to forsake the ones I love. When friends or family have seemingly strayed past hope, grant me the strength to take heart and trust in Your purposes.

I need not fear, for not only are You present in every moment I take a breath, but You are in control. I confess I do not always trust what You are doing, and for that please forgive me. Time and again You prove Your greatness and wisdom in my life. When I am tempted, Lord, help me remember how You have provided in past times. You are great and holy, and I rest in Your presence and Word. Amen.

Not Forgotten

He has sent me to bind up the brokenhearted, to proclaim
freedom for the captives and release from darkness for the prisoners.
ISAIAH 61:1 NIV

*D*ear Father, You really do care, don't You? Sometimes I feel like a prisoner in a dark room, lonely and forgotten. Everyone goes about their lives, unaware of my difficulties. But I'm not forgotten, am I? You see me. You know what I'm going through. And You care deeply.

You are working right now to deliver me from this difficult place. I have hope in You. Though the days may seem long and this journey seems endless, I know it will be okay. Right now, help me keep breathing. Keep moving. Keep accomplishing the daily tasks that are required of me. I can't do it on my own, Lord.

And I know that one day soon, I'll look up and see a beam of sunlight through a crack in the wall of my hardships. One day soon, You will arrive with a big set of keys that will set me free from this place. One day soon, my heart will be mended and I'll be able to breathe on my own again.

Thank You for seeing me, Lord. Thank You for knowing and for caring. Most of all, thank You for hope. With Your help, I can get through this. With Your help, I know I'll make it out of here to a place of freedom and blessing and peace. Amen.

A Prayer for Perseverance

*Praying always with all prayer and supplication
in the Spirit, and watching thereunto with all
perseverance and supplication for all saints.*
EPHESIANS 6:18 KJV

Lord, when things get rough and I hear about disaster and suffering around the world, I wonder if I have what it takes to make it to the end. Some people endure unspeakable sorrow and pain in their lives. Am I strong enough to stand if those things come my way?

Paul writes in Ephesians 6:13–14 to put on the whole armor of God to be able to stand in the evil day. I believe he's saying I need Your armor to persevere. Without it, I am destined to fail. Lord, dress me in Your armor. I need the strength and perseverance it takes to win the battle.

Make me strong, Lord. When I get tired, help me wait upon You as the prophet Isaiah teaches, so that my strength shall be renewed. Strengthen me that I can run and not be weary, I can walk and not faint.

Help me pray in the Spirit at all times for others that their needs and requests might be met. Help me be alert and watch for the enemy and his tricks. As I pray, may perseverance rise up in me by Your power and Your Spirit, making me the soldier I need to be for the battle ahead. Lord, I thank You for helping me to persevere now and in the future. Amen.

I Can't Fix It

Therefore humble yourselves [demote, lower yourselves in your own estimation] under the mighty hand of God, that in due time He may exalt you, casting the whole of your care [all your anxieties, all your worries, all your concerns, once and for all] on Him, for He cares for you affectionately and cares about you watchfully.

1 PETER 5:6–7 AMPC

Why is it easier to worry than to give You my concerns? I know I can't change anything by sleepless nights of anxiety, yet so often I grab my cares again after I've handed them to You.

Is it really my pride? I choose to humble myself and never try to tell You how to remedy bad situations. You've shown me so many times that You have a better plan than I could have ever come up with. Your strategy is positive for everyone concerned, while I only think of myself and the little circle of people I love. You work things out for me, and at the same time You design a perfect plan for each person. Help me remember that Your love and ability is beyond the stretch of my imagination.

Give me confidence that You care about everything going on in my life. Your affection for me won't allow anything that doesn't ultimately make me more Christlike. Thank You, Lord, for the assurance that Your mighty hand will exalt me in due time. You are awesome! Amen.

Continually with You

Nevertheless I am continually with You; You have taken
hold of my right hand. With Your counsel You will
guide me, and afterward receive me to glory.
PSALM 73:23–24 NASB

*L*ord, You are always with me. There is not a moment of my life where I will be separated from You. There is nowhere that I could run to be hidden from You. You are ever present before, behind, and around me. May I feel Your presence in a tangible way today.

You hold my hand. You walk with me through this life, not as a distant observer but as a close companion. Since I am connected to You, I need not fear that I will stumble or fall, because You will uphold and catch me. Keep me from trying to let go of Your hand, thinking that I can do this on my own.

You guide me with Your counsel. You haven't just created me and set me loose to make the most of this life. Instead, You counsel me as I walk through the difficult and wonderful times. You guide and direct me onto the path I should take. May I hear Your voice more clearly every day.

You will receive me to glory. You not only walk with me through this life, but You will hold my hand through death itself and be on the other side to receive me home. You will never, not even in death, leave or forsake me. Amen.

Help in Weakness

Also, the Spirit helps us with our weakness. We do not know how
to pray as we should. But the Spirit himself speaks to God for us,
even begs God for us with deep feelings that words cannot explain.
ROMANS 8:26 NCV

Jesus, there are times when I have no words. I have, at times, been full of so many different emotions, I don't understand myself. I don't know how to pray. Thank You for sending the Holy Spirit, my Helper, to encourage and strengthen me when I am tired, weak, and feeling defeated. When there are only tears, may those tears flow and speak for me. Tears are a language You understand, even when I don't understand them. Give me courage to trust You and speak to You from my heart with the help of the Holy Spirit. I look to Him for comfort and words. He will teach me to pray.

Sometimes I need to pray for someone else but don't know the details of their situation. Thankfully, I don't have to have any information. You know their name, their heart, and their circumstance. You know what's going on. You know what they need. I pray for them now. I lend support to them through my prayers. Speak to them; comfort them; give them wisdom and understanding. Give me Your words to speak when I see them so that I may be a help to them as well. Amen.

Don't Be. Seek Me.

Do not be anxious about anything, but in everything
by prayer and supplication with thanksgiving let
your requests be made known to God.
PHILIPPIANS 4:6 ESV

I am anxious about seemingly everything, Abba. Pull me away from myself and direct my thoughts to You. You command believers to seek Your face because fellowship with You is why we were created. From the very beginning, it is in Your presence that humans find their joy and worth. Forgive me when, like Adam, I think that I can hide from You when I put my trust in concealment and avoidance. Let me live in the truth that You see everything. You yearn to be united with Your creation—to draw us to You like a hen gathers her chicks. Oh, Abba, so much more than that, You command us to tell You what weighs down our hearts—to tell You what we want—because it brings us back to Eden.

Let Your people seek that first unspotted, pure devotion to You. Let us in joyful anticipation speak to You and wait for Your response. Strengthen us to approach You in gratitude, knowing You have it all in control. Father, we are here now, anxious and scared because our nature is affected by the fall into sin. We are here nonetheless, in obedience and expectation. As we seek to be in Your presence we feel You drawing us to the core of our being, to dependence on Your grace and Your love to provide. Amen.

A Fortified Heart

*Yet those who wait for the L*ORD *will gain new strength;*
they will mount up with wings like eagles, they will run
and not get tired, they will walk and not become weary.
ISAIAH 40:31 NASB

Almighty God, in all Your majesty and greatness, You care about each one of us. When we are hurt or frightened, You fortify us against all our worries and fears. You let us exchange our limiting weakness for Your immeasurable strength.

When foreboding comes upon us like an invading army, we will not retreat. For we know You are our shield. We confidently proclaim, " 'Behold, God is my salvation, I will trust and not be afraid; for the LORD GOD is my strength and song' " (Isaiah 12:2 NASB).

Eagles beat the air with their mighty wings to take flight, soaring over the trees, up to the mountaintops and beyond. You lift us up with the power of eagles' wings above our forests of earthly concerns. Our troubles grow smaller when we view them through Your perspective. Trees become sticks, and mountains become molehills. We can manage our troubles with Your help.

We give thanks to You, Lord, as You fortify our hearts in the midst of trepidation. You give us complete, true peace of mind in these difficult times.

As we pray in the powerful and wonderful name of Jesus, let each of us declare, "I can do all things through Him who strengthens me" (Philippians 4:13 NASB). Amen.

Just Call Me "Martha"

*"Martha, Martha," the Lord answered, "you are worried
and upset about many things, but few things are needed—
or indeed only one. Mary has chosen what is better,
and it will not be taken away from her."*
LUKE 10:41–42 NIV

Dear Jesus, I am a Martha. You know who I mean: the woman from the Bible who was too busy with life to stop and listen to You. Yes, that's me. Martha.

I always think that I have so much to do. I spend my time running around trying to get things done, and I'm often worried and anxious. Being a Martha gets in the way of my relationship with You, and I'm sorry about that, Lord.

I suppose that being a Martha isn't all bad. You loved her so much, just like You love me. And You scolded her gently when she was too busy for You—just like You are scolding me now. Thank You for being gentle with me. Thank You for reminding me to slow down and put You first.

Will You help me try harder? Too often I'm unaware that I'm so wrapped up in busyness that I've made no time for You. I want to be able to say no to tasks that pull me away from You. I want to be at peace when leaving some things undone so I can spend more time with You. Will You help me do that, Lord? Thank You so much. Amen.

God Is Our Salvation

You will say in that day: "I will give thanks to you, O Lord,
for though you were angry with me, your anger turned away,
that you might comfort me. Behold, God is my salvation;
I will trust, and will not be afraid; for the Lord God is my
strength and my song, and he has become my salvation."
Isaiah 12:1–2 esv

How mysterious and wonderful it is to serve a God who turns His anger and comforts His children. There is no other God, no one like You. I admit that it is difficult to be anxious for nothing, to set all potential worries and fears on Your altar and wait. Some of the hardest commands You give us are to wait, be still and resist. But in those days of salvation and restoration, may I praise You. May I give thanks in the sorrowful and joyful times.

Forgive me, Lord. Forgive me for defying You, clinging to my pride and denying Your holiness. You are my salvation. You are my Savior and only strength. All other avenues wring me dry and leave me beaten. Because of my pride and unbelief, I sought after my own methods of salvation. In the times when I am tempted to follow the lies, to resort to my own plans, help me trust in You and not be afraid of obedience. Thank You for turning Your anger from me. Thank You for sacrificing Your Son and forgiving me, a sinner. Amen.

Comfort Me

He has sent me. . .to proclaim the year of the Lord's favor. . .
to comfort all who mourn, and provide for those who grieve.
ISAIAH 61:1–3 NIV

*D*ear Father, life is such a series of hills and valleys, isn't it? I can be on the highest hilltop, and just like that, *boom!* Something will happen, and I'm devastated. The opposite is true too. One day it can seem like darkness is all I will ever see, when suddenly a moment of hope will pierce through the fog and I'll know something better waits in the near future.

You comfort me with Your hope, Father. When I'm mourning the loss of a loved one or a friendship or a season in life, I feel overwhelmed. When I'm at my lowest point, that's when I feel Your presence the strongest. You whisper love and kindness into my spirit, and I know You care. I know I'm not alone on this journey. Gently You point my gaze to a better time in the future, and I know I won't be in the valley forever.

You provide what I need when I'm devastated. Whether it's a cool breeze on a hot day or a phone call from a friend, You always find a way to make sure I'm cared for. Thank You for loving me with tenderness, compassion, and comfort. Thank You for hope in Your goodness. Amen.

Peace from God

*Thou wilt keep him in perfect peace, whose mind is stayed
on thee: because he trusteth in thee. Trust ye in the LORD
for ever: for in the LORD JEHOVAH is everlasting strength.*
ISAIAH 26:3–4 KJV

Lord, thank You for Your promises, which never fail. You're faithful to Your Word. I pray that I will always stand on those promises in every circumstance. That includes the promise in Isaiah 26 about the peace You give.

I confess, Lord, that my mind isn't always on You. Life gets hectic, and I admit to feeling stressed about too many situations. I need the peace only You can give. Help me trust You in every situation and allow You to solve my problems, because the only real peace that I have comes from You.

To have real peace, I need to think on those things that please You. Instead of filling my mind with images and information the world around me supplies, I need to dwell on Your goodness and the wisdom and knowledge that comes from the Holy Spirit. Increase my hunger for Your Word. Whatever I see, read, hear, or speak, let it bring You glory. For when it brings You glory, it will bring me peace.

Lord, I want to be kept in perfect peace. I ask You to transform my thinking and my desires. Help me trust You completely and keep my mind on You and Your Word. Amen.

Do Whatever It Takes, Lord

And we know that in all things God works for the good of those who love him, who have been called according to his purpose. For those God foreknew he also predestined to be conformed to the image of his Son, that he might be the firstborn among many brothers and sisters.
ROMANS 8:28–29 NIV

*P*recious Lord Jesus, that scripture is so positive, yet in the midst of trials it can be hard to believe. Please erase my doubts, Lord. Life wasn't easy for Christians when Paul wrote those words, yet he had confidence that, even when things went wrong, You would ultimately turn it into good. You see the eternal; I'm caught in this moment.

You continually transform us to look like Jesus. I want to match that image, but I'm such a chicken about going through tough times that will make me the person You plan for me to become.

I love the concept that You knew me before I was even born and predestined me to be here on earth at this precise time. You didn't force my destiny, but You knew from the beginning that I would choose to follow You. I took some wrong turns, caused problems along the way, but You are faithful and used every obstacle to put me back on the right path. You planned my life to eventually make me part of Your glorious kingdom.

I long to be more like You, Jesus, every day. Amen.

God Gives the Victory

But thanks be to God, who gives us the victory through our Lord Jesus Christ.
Therefore, my beloved brethren, be steadfast, immovable, always abounding
in the work of the Lord, knowing that your toil is not in vain in the Lord.
1 Corinthians 15:57–58 nasb

*L*ord, right now I feel anything but victorious. I am bogged down in the daily stressors of life and the fear I have about the future. I feel that I have failed in different aspects of my life and regret the way that I have handled certain situations. And yet, Lord, You tell me that through Your Son there is victory. Forgive me when I look in the wrong places for my value and my standing with You. I am covered in the righteousness of Jesus and, because of His work on the cross, will spend eternity in heaven. *That* is victory. Keep me focused on this eternal perspective when I start to pay too much attention to my shortcomings in life.

Thank You for the reassurance that when I do Your work it is not in vain. Even when I feel inadequate, You will use my efforts for the good of Your kingdom. Keep me from discouragement and weariness, and grant me strength and perseverance. Give me a cheerful and willing attitude to do Your will. May I be seeking out even more opportunities to do Your work and help others, as I know that I will be blessed in that as well. Amen.

Truth = Freedom

*"And you will know the truth,
and the truth will set you free."*
JOHN 8:32 ESV

*H*eavenly Father, there seems to always be more than one side to a story. Each person looks at life differently, from a perspective that is filtered through their own life experiences. Sometimes those filters seem positive, and sometimes they're negative, depending on how much light or truth is revealed. I want to live my life in the truth—Your truth. I want to see each person's story from Your perspective. Give me Your grace so that I may see them as You see them. Let their stories be as important to me as they are important to You.

So many times people judge me based on their own story. They don't know the reality of my experience. There are times even I am not sure I have the whole truth about my story. Help me climb above the chaos, confusion, judgment, hurt, and pain of past wounds. Help me receive Your forgiveness so that I can live in the truth and give grace to others as well.

Let all things hidden be revealed in my life. Open my eyes to see the truth—the reality of my redemption through Your love for me and for others. I open my heart to receive Your truth today. Shine Your light on all things and show me truth that I may know it and live it in a way that honors You. Amen.

Hope in Your Holy Morning

Sing praises to the LORD, O you his saints, and give thanks
to his holy name. For his anger is but for a moment, and his
favor is for a lifetime. Weeping may tarry for the night,
but joy comes with the morning.
PSALM 30:4–5 ESV

Jehovah, I sing Your praises because You count me among Your people. Your saints, those set apart, give You thanks for providing this "apartness." Though we are a piece of this disaster-filled world, You have drawn us in grace to see You work out Your redemption. Our hearts sing at the beauty of Your holiness. You are pure when everything around us is tainted. But You seek the same purity of us, and that is overwhelming. Help us remember that Your anger is just, which purifies and makes us whole. Thank You that Your anger is brief. Make us holy as You are holy, as Jesus calls us to be.

In Sabina Wurmbrand's words, help us consider this experience as the beauty parlor of God, where we come out cleaner and more beautiful than any earthly system of beautification—we come out as living saints. Give strength to your saints who are going through a night of sorrow. Bring us the joy that comes with the morning. In Your favor is life. Embolden us in obedience to Your Word and love of Your person, which produces life. You, Lord, are our perpetual morning-song and joy in the midst of suffering. Amen.

A Willing Heart

*Therefore, those also who suffer according to the will of God
shall entrust their souls to a faithful Creator in doing what is right.*
1 PETER 4:19 NASB

*R*ighteous Father, we might consider it a blessing when others berate us for our belief, if we weren't so incensed by their chiding.

The purpose of our suffering is to refine and strengthen our faith, to demonstrate our salvation by proving our fidelity. We bring honor to You, O God, when we show others You have provided the Holy Spirit to help us.

To do Your will means being prepared to die to self. Our fleshly person must give way to our spiritual one. We fight this battle daily. When the skirmish discourages us, let us remember that even Christ prayed, "Father, if You are willing, remove this cup from Me." When we pray for You to remove our own cup of suffering, remind us of His conclusion to that prayer: ". . .yet not My will, but Yours be done" (Luke 22:42 NASB). We share Christ's suffering because we willingly bear His name.

It's difficult to do Your will when Satan strikes out at us for choosing to follow Jesus' path. Help us remember to entrust our souls to our faithful Creator and do what is right. Let Your will be done, whether we face adversity or pleasure. Then we can say, "I delight to do Your will, O my God; Your Law is within my heart" (Psalm 40:8 NASB). Amen.

Oh, Great and Mighty God

The mountains melt like wax before the LORD,
before the Lord of all the earth.
PSALM 97:5 NIV

Kind heavenly Father, when I feel like I'm in a valley surrounded by mountains of trouble, I remember Your greatness. The mountains close me in and look impossible to climb. I wish to get over them to the other side, but I am powerless to scale them without You.

I know that somehow You will lift me up and over the highest peak and set me safely on the other side. You are so great.

God, You are so good. Your Word teaches me that when I walk through a valley I needn't be afraid, because You are with me. You give me hope. There is nothing too big for You, no trouble too great. Your Word says that You can make mountains melt like wax because You are Lord of all the earth. Just knowing that brings me comfort.

Father, give me peace in this valley while I wait. Ease my mind. Increase my faith, and enlighten me with hopeful scriptures. Make me intensely aware of Your presence. Encourage me to listen for Your voice and to recognize when You urge me to act. I know, Father, that this valley is temporary. I believe with all my heart that You have something wonderful waiting for me on the other side of the mountains. So come, great and mighty God. Come and lift me up. Amen.

Smaller Than a Mustard Seed

Then Job answered the Lord and said: "I know that you can
do all things, and that no purpose of yours can be thwarted."
JOB 42:1–2 ESV

*D*o I live in the knowledge that You, Lord, can do all things? Or do I walk each day hesitantly, as though You will not provide or will not answer my call? So very often I doubt, and my faith is small. How is it that I can worship such a great, vast God and have a tiny belief?

When You are not preeminent in my life, problems become foremost and all circumstances overwhelm me. I sink further into hopelessness and all the loveliness of Christ and the Gospel fades to shadows. I seem to be losing every battle, but that is because I trust in my own strength, which is a brittle stick to Your mountainous might.

Forgive my unbelief, Lord. It robs You of Your glory and it chains me to insecurity. There is nothing more powerful than You, Lord, but do I live as though this is truth? I store so much knowledge of Your Word and promises in my head, but I never let them settle and grow in my heart. I keep them stashed away as nice facts that I can access when sorrow sets in, like aspirin for muscle pain, but I do not live by them. Lord, help me place them as a seal in my heart. Help me bind them around my neck so that I am ever conscious of You. Amen.

Beauty for Ashes

*He has sent me. . .to bestow on them a crown of beauty
instead of ashes, the oil of joy instead of mourning,
and a garment of praise instead of a spirit of despair.*
ISAIAH 61:1, 3 NIV

Dear Father, right now my life feels like ashes, mourning and despair. I try to have a positive outlook, but it's hard when things just keep getting worse. I'm afraid there will be no end to the sadness. That anxiety affects everything. My stomach hurts. I can't sleep. It's difficult to accomplish even small tasks.

But, Father, You know all that, don't You? You know everything about me, and You promised not to leave me alone. You walk with me through the desolation. And You assure me that if I'll just stick with You, You'll lead me to a much better season.

Father, my hope is in You. I know that, despite my current state, You're taking me to a place of joy and beauty and happiness. Help me clear my tears enough to notice the sweet blessings You lay in my path.

Each time I feel anxious, remind me to focus on the promises of this verse. Gladness, praise, and beauty are in store for me, along with Your never-ending love and faithfulness. Thank You for the good things You have for me. I love You, and I trust You. Amen.

Do All for God's Glory

Let the message of Christ dwell among you richly as
you teach and admonish one another with all wisdom
through psalms, hymns, and songs from the Spirit, singing
to God with gratitude in your hearts. And whatever you
do, whether in word or deed, do it all in the name of the
Lord Jesus, giving thanks to God the Father through him.
COLOSSIANS 3:16–17 NIV

Thank You, Father, for the message of Christ. Thank You for filling us with Your Spirit and giving the psalms, hymns, and songs that teach and bless us so richly. May we always use what You have given us to bring glory to Your name.

Father, I ask that the message of Christ take precedence in my life so that whatever I do, I can do it in wisdom and love. Let me not do anything for recognition or glory, but so others can know You. When I speak, write, or sing, let me do it out of a grateful heart for Your blessings in my life. As Your Word says: it's in You that we live, move, and have our being. The gifts and benefits I enjoy would not be possible without You. May every deed I undertake be done with the proper motive—to bring glory to Your name.

Father, purify my thoughts and motives so people will see You, not me, and give You honor. Give me a song in my heart and help me sing it with gratitude to You. Amen.

I'm Safe in You

"No weapon forged against you will prevail, and you will refute every tongue that accuses you. This is the heritage of the servants of the LORD, and this is their vindication from me," declares the LORD.
ISAIAH 54:17 NIV

What fantastic assurance that scripture gives me, Lord. Thank You for inviting me into the safety of Your presence, where I can be safe from attacks of the enemy. Satan's weapons are harmless when I take refuge in You.

Whether it's unkind words, plots to cause me harm, or false accusations, I can be confident when I stay close to You. Those weapons won't prevail; You put perfect words in my mouth to refute any lies. You will shelter me from the ugliness of life if I allow You to do as You wish. Sometimes I forget. I step away from Your protective cover and try to fight my own battles, but that is always wrong and leads to confusion. I need Your constant protection, and You are always there to provide it.

When I consider the heritage that has been passed on to me because I'm Your servant, I can only bow my heart in total humility. I haven't earned Your protection or vindication. You freely give everything we need to each person who reaches out to You. You provide the weapons and armor for us to fight our battles and come through them unscathed.

Being Your servant is an awesome privilege. Thank You, Lord. Amen.

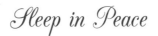

Sleep in Peace

In peace I will both lie down and sleep,
for You alone, O LORD, make me to dwell in safety.
PSALM 4:8 NASB

Lord, You alone are my safety. No security system or retirement plan or top-safety rated car is responsible for my safety. You are the One in control of every aspect of my life.

Under Your protection there is true peace. I can put my life and the lives of those I love in Your hands, as the sovereign God of the universe, in complete confidence that nothing will happen to us that is outside of Your will. But not only are You sovereign; You are also good and You love me. I can, therefore, be sure that even the most difficult of circumstances are not out of Your control and will somehow, now or in the future, be worked out for my good and the good of others.

Because You are sovereign, good, and loving, I can sleep in peace.

I need not lie awake at night thinking through everything I need to do or should have done. It is all in Your hands, anyway. I relinquish the worry that I have been holding about my life over to You now. I ask that You will give me peace about each circumstance and help me see that You are in control.

Grant me a peaceful and secure sleep tonight, knowing that You will make me dwell in safety. Amen.

Lead Me in Peace

You will keep in perfect peace those whose minds
are steadfast, because they trust in you.
Isaiah 26:3 niv

Lord, I trust You. You are my comfort and my peace. On days like today, there is so much noise inside my head. Creative ideas, worries, concerns, solutions, possibilities shout at me from within. Just the day-to-day living can stress me out, and I find it difficult to become quiet; it's hard for me to pray.

But I think of Your peace, the quietness of a stream of the living water You are pouring out to me. I focus on Your love for me. I remember Your words; You are my Good Shepherd and You lead me. You give me what I need. All I have to do is follow You. Help me relax and lean on You. I will follow You because You are my life. You know where I need to go. I turn my thoughts to You. I shut the rest of the noise out.

Strengthen me and help me not to become overwhelmed. I can have a heart filled with peace with Your help. I set my mind on You and release all that concerns me into Your capable hands. I refuse to be fearful or nervous and, instead, trust You to work it all out. You have never failed me, and You won't fail me now. You are my peace! I close my eyes and rest in You now. Amen.

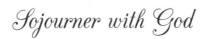

Sojourner with God

Therefore, as you received Christ Jesus the Lord, so walk
in him, rooted and built up in him and established in the faith,
just as you were taught, abounding in thanksgiving.
COLOSSIANS 2:6–7 ESV

God of my path, I have received Jesus as Lord of my life and Savior of my soul. Help me walk with Him as my guide and with the Trinity as my ever-present companion. Root me in the truth that Jesus came to save and heal all that is broken in creation and that He is the manifestation of You—of Your love—incarnate. Make the root of this truth sprout abounding love in me to conquer my selfish thoughts and worried heart. Build me up in the power of Christ to grow strong in my knowledge of His teachings and in living out His words. Fashion in me the characteristics of Your Son, the second Adam, and in Jesus may I hope to return to the state of the first Adam before the fall. Equip me to hold fast to my confession of faith, to remain steadfast in my belief as I recall what the Spirit has taught me and as I trust that You accept my prayers brought to You by my forever-interceding High Priest. In the act of remembering what I learned and in continuing the process, I am inundated with a spirit of thanks. Push me to "continue steadfastly in prayer, being watchful in it with thanksgiving" (Colossians 4:2 ESV). Amen.

A Disciplined Heart

For they disciplined us for a short time as seemed best to them,
but He disciplines us for our good, so that we may share His holiness.
HEBREWS 12:10 NASB

Oh Lord, my God, too often I become so focused on my struggles that I forget to look for the benefits veiled beneath them. A rebuke doesn't seem like a blessing until I scrutinize the fundamental root of my situation.

As difficult as it is to admit, I am thankful for Your chastening. When my misguided decisions pull me away from You, I come face-to-face with regret and, sometimes, grief. Then I remember Your words: "All discipline for the moment seems not to be joyful, but sorrowful; yet to those who have been trained by it, afterwards it yields the peaceful fruit of righteousness" (Hebrews 12:11 NASB).

You rebuke, reprove, and instruct me because You love me. I am Your child. Those moments bring discomfort or heartache at first. But then I look back and see Your loving hand guiding me back to the path of righteousness—back to You, dear Father.

What a wonderful blessing to know, as Your child, it is for discipline that I endure. And being Your child, I can come straight to You in my times of need, even when the dilemma is for my own growth. Thank You for loving me enough to chastise me and give me a disciplined heart for You.

In Jesus' name, amen.

Trouble at Work

I can do all things through Christ who strengthens me.
PHILIPPIANS 4:13 NKJV

*D*ear Lord, thank You for my job. I appreciate the work that You have given me and the income that it provides. But, Lord, I have trouble at work, and Your Word teaches that I should bring everything to You in prayer, all my needs.

You know about the pressure that I am facing and the stress it brings. There are days when I feel like quitting. Sometimes I question my ability to do my job well. The workload is heavy, and I wonder if I am strong enough to carry it. I also wonder if I am where You want me to be, or if I should move on.

Lord, please help me have a right attitude about my work and those in authority. Help me endure the pressure and do my job well. Also, give me strength to accept the workload and get the job done. I need Your wisdom. Am I in the right job? Am I where You want me to be? Lead me and show me the way.

I want to remember to work as if I am working for You—because I am! I want to do my job in a way that pleases You, and I want my attitude to reflect who You are. I want others to see You through me and my work. So help me please, dear Lord. Amen.

Song in the Night

"Let me remember my song in the night; let me meditate in my heart." Then my spirit made a diligent search.

Psalm 77:6 esv

Lord, there are times, such as now, that I do not feel like searching for You or entering Your presence. I do not have the time, but that is a poor excuse and a slap in the face to the God of the universe. I yearn to do other things than read Your Word, meditate on scripture, or talk to You. Yet slowly like a frantic heartbeat steadies, You draw me into Your embrace and I begin to meditate on Your song and words.

I think of Your goodness in times of financial abundance and drought, of relationship joys and pain. When it comes to decisions, especially financial, I present the concern to You, yet I already have a solution in my head, and if Your answer does not line up with my solution, I grow skeptical and unbelieving. Lord, forgive me for being so inflexible and unwilling to obey or listen. How can I call myself a faithful child and follower when my heart and mind are hostile toward all Your guidance? Forgive me for lashing out at others, for my unbelief in You. Lord, mold me to Your will; make me clay in Your hands. You have provided countless times, from weekly groceries to healed friendships. Thank You for the great adventure of knowing You and growing in You. Amen.

Master Builder

They will rebuild the ancient ruins and restore the places long devastated; they will renew the ruined cities that have been devastated for generations.
ISAIAH 61:4 NIV

*D*ear Father, thank You for this verse, this promise to Your people. I know it refers to the nation of Israel, but it is also a promise about my life. In this verse, there is hope. In this verse, I find reason to let go of my fears and focus on a beautiful future, in You.

Many areas of my life feel like they're already in ruin, or about to be. Relationships are damaged, and I worry they won't ever be mended. Things are broken and crumbled, and it seems they'll never be repaired. But according to this scripture, You're going to put it all back together.

Father, You are the Master Architect of my life. You built it, but sin and others' actions and my own choices have caused a lot of damage. But since You created me in the first place, I know You have the power to recreate and rebuild and restore what's been lost. Instead of focusing my thoughts on the destruction, help me set my mind on the current construction that's taking place. I know You're working behind the scenes to fashion something beautiful and wholesome, something even better than I can imagine. Thank You for Your divine design in my life, Father. Amen.

A Prayer When You Are Troubled

*Listen to my prayer, O God, do not ignore my plea; hear me and
answer me. My thoughts trouble me and I am distraught because of
what my enemy is saying, because of the threats of the wicked; for they
bring down suffering on me and assail me in their anger. . . . Cast your cares
on the LORD and he will sustain you; he will never let the righteous be shaken.*

PSALM 55:1–3, 22 NIV

Lord, I confess I am troubled about what's happening around me. I don't like the things I hear others saying and see them doing. Please give me an answer to these troubling thoughts. I'm uneasy when I'm at odds with others, but I know I must answer for my own actions and words, not theirs.

We live in a world where frightening events are happening every day. It troubles me that evil is so prevalent, good people are not respected, and families are so distant. I need Your help to remember that You are in control. Help me not to be afraid of what people say to me or threaten to do when they disagree with me. Whatever I face, I know You stand beside me. I am not alone.

Lord, take my cares. I give them to You. Sustain me through the bad times. Thank You for the promise that You will not allow me to lose my footing but will keep me on solid ground, unshaken. Amen.

My High Tower

The Lord also will be a refuge and a high tower for
the oppressed, a refuge and a stronghold in times
of trouble (high cost, destitution, and desperation).
PSALM 9:9 AMPC

*D*ear heavenly Father, thank You for being a refuge for me when things go wrong. I can run to You, my High Tower, where I'm safe and secure in the midst of a desperate situation. I picture a stronghold, like a fortress or castle, where I'm sheltered behind strong walls so nothing can harm me.

We all face times when we feel destitute, and even if there were some way to get help, the high cost would be beyond our ability. But You are there for us, to provide for all our needs, without expecting any payback. We can never repay You for the protection You give, and we don't need to. All You ask is that we give our hearts—our entire lives are completely for You.

Nothing I can offer is equal to the value of what You give, yet You are always ready to protect me. I need to be just as eager to ask for Your help as You are to offer it. You see my desperation even before I realize I'm heading into a desperate spot. You prepare my help right then, and as soon as I cry out to You, a safe refuge is ready and waiting.

Let me run to You without any delay. You are my stronghold. Amen.

You Know All My Ways

O Lord, You have searched me and known me. You know when I sit down and when I rise up; You understand my thought from afar. You scrutinize my path and my lying down, and are intimately acquainted with all my ways. Even before there is a word on my tongue, behold, O Lord, You know it all. You have enclosed me behind and before, and laid Your hand upon me.
PSALM 139:1–5 NASB

Lord, even though the fact that You see and know everything that I do and think is somewhat intimidating, it is also wonderfully comforting. I can't accidentally stray from the course that I should be following without You noticing. You don't forget about me or allow me to make mistakes because You were looking the other way. Instead, You are intimately aware of each moment of my life. Since You know all that I do, I can trust You completely to guide me and direct me in the way I should go.

I am so humbled that You would have such an interest in me to actually care about what I do on a daily basis. I do not need to be concerned that my prayers bother or inconvenience You, because You are already paying attention to me before I even speak a word of petition. What peace I can have knowing that not one step that I take will be outside of Your watchful and loving gaze. Amen.

Holding Tight to God for My Future

"For I know the plans I have for you," says the LORD.
"They are plans for good and not for disaster,
to give you a future and a hope."
JEREMIAH 29:11 NLT

God, You created me for success. You want the best for me, and You've set that plan in motion. I've been so busy chasing my future, trying to make things happen in my time, that I forget sometimes to ask You what is best. Once I ask, I need to listen to You and follow Your direction. Forgive me for the times I've come up with a plan, put it into action, and then prayed for You to bless it. Your plans for my life are so much more than I could ask or imagine.

There's a struggle in my mind for control of my future. It can be a scary feeling to let go, but I know faith calls for me to live one day at a time following Your lead. Give me courage and strength today to let go of control and, instead, hold tight to You. I will trust You each day with my future. Remind me through Your Word that I don't have to worry or wonder about my future. You have set me on a course. I will listen as You speak to my heart. Direct my life and show me the future You have designed for me. I trust You for an amazing future. Amen.

The Lord's Comfort in Zion

*"Listen to me, you who pursue righteousness, you who
seek the Lord: look to the rock from which you were hewn,
and to the quarry from which you were dug."*

ISAIAH 51:1 ESV

God who pleads the cause of His people, thank You for providing a way out of darkness for those who pursue You as Truth. Our ears are open. Speak to us. You draw us to look to our source, to see how You made Abraham a mighty people because his faith was regarded as righteousness. From elderly Sarah you brought a son of laughter—joy in Your love and hope in Your promise. Turn the desert of my circumstance into Your garden where I can walk with You in friendship. Fill this period with joy in my interactions with family and friends and with gladness to serve those in the church and my colleagues at work or school. I cling to Your promise of producing thanksgiving, and may my voice turn to songs of praise even in the midst of pressure.

I praise You that Your justice is light to the nations and that Your salvation is forever. You have promised to buy back Your people from slavery to sin. The picture You paint is beautiful: we will return to You with singing. Your everlasting joy will pour over us, and it already is, if we would open our hearts to feel it. You, our Rock and our support, are our source and comfort. Amen.

A Steadfast Heart

"The steadfast of mind You will keep in
perfect peace, because he trusts in You."
ISAIAH 26:3 NASB

*D*ear Lord Jesus, You never change. You are the same yesterday, today, and tomorrow. From everlasting to everlasting is Your love for us.

But we change every day. From infancy to adulthood, our bodies undergo a physical metamorphosis. Then our bodies grow old. We gain and lose weight. Our knowledge, attitudes, and opinions shift as our minds develop and mature. Even our faith in You can change with blessings or struggles, hopefully deepening in strength and not diminishing from weariness.

Your Word gives us the strength to contend with the negatives the world hurls at us. "Therefore, my beloved brethren, be steadfast, immovable, always abounding in the work of the Lord, knowing that your toil is not in vain in the Lord" (1 Corinthians 15:58 NASB). As we trust in our unchanging Savior, we can continue to do Your good work, knowing it is not in vain. Clinging to our immovable faith, Your perfect peace will never leave us. Our anxious thoughts don't stand a chance against Your calming Spirit.

We find hope in Your steadfast love and look forward to the time when our perishable existence will put on the imperishable of eternity with You. What is sown in dishonor will be raised in glory. What is sown in weakness will be raised in power. We will never change again. Amen.

When the World Gets Me Down

Don't copy the behavior and customs of this world,
but let God transform you into a new person by changing
the way you think. Then you will learn to know God's
will for you, which is good and pleasing and perfect.
ROMANS 12:2 NLT

*D*ear Lord, when the world gets me down, I'm so grateful to know that You are in control. The television, newspapers, and Internet are filled with news of Satan's victories. But they aren't victories, not really, because Your goodness shines through as Your people rise above pain and tragedy and give You the glory. Satan never wins. Goodness always comes on the heels of evil as individuals help each other and work to make the world a better place.

When the world gets me down, I will not give in or give up! Lord, this is what You taught us to do: to persevere in the face of adversity and to hold tight to our faith. When the world is worrisome, You remind us that we are not of this world. We belong to You, and one day You will come to wage a great war against evil. And You will win! You always win. So when the world gets me down, I will remember that.

Lord, keep my eyes open to Your goodness all around me, and give me strength in adversity. Thank You for all that You are and all that You do. I love You, Lord. Amen.

Songs of Strength

Each evening they come back, howling like dogs and prowling about the city. They wander about for food and growl if they do not get their fill. But I will sing of your strength; I will sing aloud of your steadfast love in the morning. For you have been to me a fortress and a refuge in the day of my distress.
PSALM 59:14–16 ESV

Though my worries, fears, and enemies seem as constant as the rising sun, Lord, You are more steadfast. You are more steadfast than the coming of rain in the spring, the silent fall of snow in winter, the lazy heat of summer, and changing leaves in autumn. You are sovereign over my life and the lives of those around me. There is not one thought or breath that You do not watch. My anxieties and sorrows are not dismissed by You. You turn Your ear to my words, and though at times it doesn't feel like You listen, Your Spirit walks every step of this weary road with me. Thank You that even in the darkest and most deserted times You are my refuge.

Lord, comfort my heart. I have tried numerous remedies to soothe my nerves and they all leave me hollow as a weathered stump. Forgive me for not seeking You; You are the Creator of peace, order, and solace. Lord, You are my place of rest; may I abide in Your Word and presence each day. May I hunger for Your hand in my life, and search for more ways to praise You. Amen.

A Prayer to Increase Faith

*Now faith is the substance of things hoped for, the evidence of
things not seen. For by it the elders obtained a good report. . . .
These all died in faith, not having received the promises,
but having seen them afar off, and were persuaded of them,
and embraced them, and confessed that they were
strangers and pilgrims on the earth.*
HEBREWS 11:1–2, 13 KJV

*L*ord, thank You for the faith of those Bible elders such as Noah and Abraham and the early Christians in the book of Acts. Their stories challenge and convict us to walk in faith. According to Hebrews 11, they obtained a good report.

Lord, increase my faith. As I read the account in Hebrews of those strong people who heard Your voice and followed You without reservation, I know I'm lacking in that area. You haven't asked me to build an ark like Noah or fight a battle like Gideon, but I feel You nudging me to draw closer to You for whatever task You have for me. Strengthen the measure of faith You have given me so I may hear You speak and follow without hesitation.

Thank You, Lord, for the faith that subdues kingdoms, obtains promises, and stops the mouth of lions. Help me be open to this kind of faith. Let my faith increase so that, when the lion does roar or the battle gets rough, I won't be afraid. Help me live by faith in You. Amen.

Humility in Anxiety

Humble yourselves, therefore, under the mighty hand of God so that at the proper time he may exalt you, casting all your anxieties on him, because he cares for you. Be sober-minded; be watchful. Your adversary the devil prowls around like a roaring lion, seeking someone to devour. Resist him, firm in your faith, knowing that the same kinds of suffering are being experienced by your brotherhood throughout the world.

1 PETER 5:6–9 ESV

God of the meek, make me humble. I want to be exalted, recognized by You and not by the fleeting exaltations of human praises. Only in humbly recognizing my shortcomings can I even attempt to realize how lavishly merciful You are. I believe that You are a God of grace who is not only powerful enough to carry my problems but commands me to give them all to You out of Your love for me. I throw all my anxieties to You.

Help me remain watchful and diligent in lifting these problems to You so that I can resist the devil through the power of faith. Remind me that fellow believers around the world are also experiencing the same kinds of suffering. Show me my weakness so that I may see Your strength all the more magnificently and not try to wriggle out of my anxieties on my own. I look to the promise of forever glory in Jesus, who will Himself restore, confirm, strengthen, and establish me. Amen.

His Plans Are Perfect

"For I know the plans I have for you," declares the LORD,
"plans to prosper you and not to harm you,
plans to give you hope and a future."
JEREMIAH 29:11 NIV

I can't grasp how You can make plans for all of us, Lord, but Your Word says it, so I believe it. It reminds me how special each person is to You—we're all vital in the great scheme of the universe. If You didn't care about us so much, You wouldn't design our lives to give us hope and a future.

Things don't happen by chance. You arrange where we live, which people touch our lives, and what we will accomplish. If we fail, You don't give up. You merely rearrange events to bring us back to the place we need to be.

I long to fit perfectly into Your purpose for my life, to please You by doing precisely what You tell me. Give me ears to hear Your voice and a heart to obey as soon as I know what I'm to do. I trust You totally, heavenly Father, knowing You see the entire scope of eternity. You know how to weave all our experiences and the events of our lives together to make each of us exactly the people we are to become.

We can only see our past and present. You are preparing a glorious future, better than our most exquisite imagination. Thank You! Amen.

The Throne of Grace

*For we do not have a high priest who cannot sympathize with our weaknesses,
but One who has been tempted in all things as we are, yet without sin. Therefore
let us draw near with confidence to the throne of grace, so that we may
receive mercy and find grace to help in time of need.*

HEBREWS 4:15–16 NASB

*L*ord, I draw near to Your throne now with confidence and lay before You all my anxiety, sadness, and fear. I ask that You would grant me the mercy and grace that You promise in these verses.

Thank You, Lord, that You are not a God that cannot understand my weakness, fear, and worry. Instead, You lived on earth and experienced all the emotions and difficulties that I am dealing with. I have a Priest and Mediator in heaven that can sympathize with my struggles. Therefore, I really can come to You with confidence, knowing that my prayers will not fall on deaf ears. Christ will hear my prayers with sympathy and will know exactly what I need to get through any struggle that I am facing, because He experienced the struggles of this world as well.

Thank You that Your throne is one of grace. It is not the throne of judgment or of aloofness. You sit on Your throne as a loving King who offers grace to those who come to You. I ask that You would shower that grace on me now as I stand before Your throne. Amen.

Believe It Until You See It

Now faith is the assurance of things hoped for,
the conviction of things not seen.
HEBREWS 11:1 ESV

*L*ord, there's a battle going on in my heart and mind. I want to believe; I want to see You in the middle of my circumstances. I want to believe the invisible. I fight against what my five physical senses tell me each day, as I endeavor to trust You to turn things around. Why is it so hard? I want to put all my confidence in Your promises, I really do. But there is a part of me that becomes afraid of hurt or disappointment. When fear tries to take up residency in my heart, help me believe You. Infuse me with Your strength and power in the middle of those doubtful thoughts.

Thank You for the many examples written in the Bible that demonstrate Your faithfulness to come through for me. I refuse to allow fear to stop me from accomplishing my God-given purpose. I will depend on You and trust You to do all You have promised. When my physical senses refuse to support what I am believing You for, I will remind myself of the times I trusted You and You came through. I continue to hope in You and believe until I see Your promises—my prayers answered and my faith to deliver, making it a reality! Amen.

David, Play on Your Harp

O Lᴏʀᴅ, rebuke me not in your anger, nor discipline me in your wrath. Be gracious to me, O Lord, for I am languishing; heal me, O Lᴏʀᴅ, for my bones are troubled. My soul also is greatly troubled. But you, O Lᴏʀᴅ—how long? Turn, O Lᴏʀᴅ, deliver my life; save me for the sake of your steadfast love. For in death there is no remembrance of you; in Sheol who will give you praise?
Psᴀʟᴍ 6:1–5 ᴇsv

*M*y great Healer and Deliverer, how long, Lord, will Your saints suffer? I turn to the prayers of David and see a restless heart that knew how to come to You. In his error he asked for mercy, and I do the same, knowing that You generously pour it out on repentant believers. David had frightening problems in his nation, in his family, and within his own heart—just as believers experience today. Yet he sang his worries to You. In my restlessness, let me find peace in Your awareness and action. Guide me to inexplicable joy in You, despite my circumstances, because of Your steadfast love. My bones and my soul may be troubled, but I trust that as You answered David, You continue to answer the cries of Your children. You have heard my plea and You accept my prayer. I sing Your praises. Whether in death or in life You do what is good, and I find peace in this trust. Amen.

The Hospitable Heart

Rejoicing in hope, persevering in tribulation, devoted to prayer,
contributing to the needs of the saints, practicing hospitality.
ROMANS 12:12–13 NASB

Almighty God, when our loved ones' souls are sick with worry or hurt from an unkind word or deed, let us be Your instruments of hope. Help us recognize Your prompting and heed Your guidance. As You have provided hospitals for physical ailments and injuries, we want to be Your spiritual hospitals.

Give us the confidence to point these heartbroken people toward You in our devotion to prayer. As You answer our prayers, they will see the power of Your love and restoration. You are the Great Physician who brings healing to our bodies and souls. Healing appears in many forms. Most often it comes in the tender heart of forgiveness and acceptance.

Practicing hospitality will take our focus off our own worries. How can we remain anxious when we're contributing to the needs of the saints? Our perseverance in tribulation will teach us compassion for others. We learn to "put on a heart of compassion, kindness, humility, gentleness and patience" (Colossians 3:12 NASB).

We are truly serving You, Lord, when we tend to the needs of those hurting in our midst. Let them see Your unfailing love through our service, rejoicing in hope that comes only from You.

We pray this in the healing name of Jesus. Amen.

When I Feel Sick

In my distress I called to the LORD; I cried to my
God for help. From his temple he heard my voice;
my cry came before him, into his ears.
PSALM 18:6 NIV

Father, I'm concerned about my health. When I feel sick, I worry that there might be something seriously wrong with my body. It's easy for me to let my imagination go wild, and I need Your help with that.

You provide me with all the tools that I need for wellness: a healthy diet, rest, exercise, and especially faith in You. Doctors can provide health and healing through Your grace, and, of course, You have the power to heal anyone of anything without human help. So why do I worry so much?

Heavenly Father, when I feel sick and come to You for help, I know that You hear me. I have no doubt that You love me and want me to be well. In sickness and in health You are my advocate, my hope, and my strength. I need to remember that You have provided me with this body, but I am not my body. The essence of who I am is my soul, and my soul is well—You created it, You saved it through Your Son's death and resurrection. My soul will never die.

So I will not worry! Instead, I will do my best to be healthy, and I will keep a positive attitude, putting my trust in You. Amen.

The First Shepherd

*Behold, the Lord God comes with might, and his arm rules
for him; behold, his reward is with him, and his recompense
before him. He will tend his flock like a shepherd; he will
gather the lambs in his arms; he will carry them in his
bosom, and gently lead those that are with young.*
ISAIAH 40:10–11 ESV

How many times have I read a passage of scripture and skipped over the descriptions of You? It is true that I pick out the passages about what You do for me, but I have never truly paused to meditate on Your character. If I desire Your nearness and a relationship with You, if I strive to build and grow my knowledge of You, then I need to seek You in the scriptures. What does this passage reveal about You?

Lord, You are not a weak God. Your justice and strength are evident throughout creation and within the hearts of Your children. Only a mighty, fearless, and merciful God would enter and bring forth healing to angry, bitter, and broken lives.

When I realize that I worship the God who measures the mountains on a scale and uproots tyrants with a brush of His hand, it amazes me. Yet, at the same time You are the God who draws lambs close and comforts the frayed hearts of Your flock. I want to know this God more. I want to study, walk, and converse with Him. This Great Shepherd who sent His Son to gather the flock back to Himself—this God intrigues me and pulls at the chords of my heart, drawing me near. Amen.

Hope in You

"Those who hope in me will not be disappointed."
ISAIAH 49:23 NIV

*D*ear Father, *hope* is a funny little word. Just four letters that can change a life. Hope is the heartfelt belief that good things will happen. It is the opposite of another four-letter word: *fear.*

So much of my life has been ruled by fear, the belief that something bad will happen. I think fear is my default setting; I unconsciously assume the worst. I'm not sure why my mind works that way, but most of the things I've worried about have not come to pass. Even when bad things do happen, they're rarely as bad as I thought they'd be.

The problem is, I can't truly enjoy the good things You place in my path because I'm too busy obsessing over the bad things that might happen. I need to change my mind's automatic response, but I don't know how. I want hope, not fear, to drive my beliefs.

Each time I find myself assuming the worst, Father, remind me of Your hope. Help me shift my thoughts to the promise of Your goodness. I want to envision my life overflowing with love and peace and joy. I'll picture relationships mended, a life rebuilt, and beautiful new beginnings. I'll trust You to bring every good thing to pass, in its proper time. I know when I hope in You that I will not be disappointed. Amen.

Don't Worry about the Future

"Do not let your hearts be troubled. You believe in God; believe also in me.
My Father's house has many rooms; if that were not so, would I have told you that
I am going there to prepare a place for you? And if I go and prepare a place for you,
I will come back and take you to be with me that you also may be where I am."
JOHN 14:1–3 NIV

Lord, I believe in You. Sometimes the devil tries to make me doubt Your Word and Your promises, but I know they are true. When my heart is troubled, speak to me and remind me of Your promise of a future home with You.

When I listen to the news and watch events unfolding around the world, I am uncertain about what will happen to our country, which in turn makes me concerned for our city and state. I pray for our leaders that they will use wisdom to direct our government and will turn their eyes upon You and Your Word.

Your Word tells me that, as a Christian, I don't need to be troubled about these things. You have taken care of the future. You have prepared a place for those who trust in You. Thank You for loving us enough to take care of our future.

Father, calm my troubled spirit and help me rest in You and Your promises. Let me not be afraid of the future. Amen.

You Did It for Your Enemies

But God showed his great love for us by sending Christ to die for us while we were still sinners. And since we have been made right in God's sight by the blood of Christ, he will certainly save us from God's condemnation. For since our friendship with God was restored by the death of his Son while we were still his enemies, we will certainly be saved through the life of his Son.

ROMANS 5:8–10 NLT

What You did for me on the cross is beyond my understanding, Lord Jesus! I didn't deserve anything, but You gave the most magnificent gift of all time—Your precious life. You saw a world of lost sinners who deserved to be condemned, but You took our condemnation. How can anyone ignore such an act of extreme compassion? I would never have admitted to being Your enemy, but in my ignorance and pride, I didn't realize my enormous need.

What can I do to show You how much I value what You did? All You ask is for me to love You in return. Such a simple request! And yet how often I go about my life as though I've accomplished something worthwhile, and pay so little attention to You. Please forgive me, Lord, though I don't deserve forgiveness or any other benefits from You. What I deserve doesn't seem to matter. All that matters is Your incredible love and mercy. You're amazing, Lord. Amen.

Strength in Weakness

And He has said to me, "My grace is sufficient for you, for power is perfected in weakness." Most gladly, therefore, I will rather boast about my weaknesses, so that the power of Christ may dwell in me. Therefore I am well content with weaknesses, with insults, with distresses, with persecutions, with difficulties, for Christ's sake; for when I am weak, then I am strong.
2 CORINTHIANS 12:9–10 NASB

*L*ord, help me grasp this remarkable concept in the same way that Paul did in these verses. It is when I am weak that Your power can be the most clearly manifested in me.

I am weak. I am going through difficulties that sap my strength. I often feel inadequate and just would like to give up. In these situations, help me be "well content" as Paul was. May I even boast in my weaknesses so that I can be a testimony to others of how Your strength is the only thing that keeps me going.

Remind me on a daily basis that Your power dwells in me. The same power that created the world and that raised Jesus from the dead *dwells in me.* There is no greater power on earth, and it is offered to me. What a resource I have that I so often overlook.

Thank You for the weaknesses and inadequacies that I have, for it's when I am weak that I can feel and display Your strength more clearly. Amen.

Inexhaustible Strength

*"The thief comes only to steal and kill and destroy.
I came that they may have life and have it abundantly."*
JOHN 10:10 ESV

*J*esus, I am tired of the lies. The enemy of my soul—the devil—brings lies, half-truths, and guilt, trying to convince me that You are not all-powerful. He tries to steal my faith with fear as his weapon. But You came to give me life and the ability to live with Your power and strength.

I am not created to house a spirit of fear but to house a spirit of power, filled with love and complete soundness of mind. The word *power* is translated in this verse as the inexhaustible strength that comes from God. So when the devil comes to try to steal from me, bring this word to my heart and mind. I have Your inexhaustible strength residing within me. I can overcome.

When the enemy reminds me that I can't erase my past, I will remember that You have erased my sin. You don't speak to me from the point of my past mistakes but from a place of freedom. Help me learn from my past and move forward. I am forgiven and free from condemnation. My future—today and for all eternity—is not based on how many times I failed or succeeded. It is, instead, based on my relationship with You. Thank You for forgiving me and for filling me with Your inexhaustible strength. Amen.

Watchmen for the Morning

I wait for the Lord, my soul waits, and in his word I hope;
my soul waits for the Lord more than watchmen for the
morning, more than watchmen for the morning.
PSALM 130:5–6 ESV

Great Morning Star, for me to remain vigilant through the darkness is at times unbearably hard. I am weary of the fight to stay awake and aware. Other times the dangers of the night produce an overwhelming fear in me. But I wait for You, Abba God. I wait because with You there is forgiveness, there is ever-faithful love, and there is hope. I know that my waiting is not passive but filled with vibrancy as I spend time in prayer and in reading Your Word. You are present always through the Holy Spirit, but it is Your acts of redemption that I long to see.

In times of deepest trials, it is in waiting for Your hand to work by which I combat my apprehensive spirit. Cultivate in me persistence to listen for Your voice during life's dark nights. Form my eyes to look for Your presence and to recognize Your touch. The psalmist writes that You offer plentiful redemption, and though I have experienced Your liberating work in my heart through the sacrifice of Jesus, I yearn for the final redemption. I yearn to see the Bridegroom return. So I will wait. Help me do so more expectantly and actively than even night watchmen, obeying and remaining in constant communication with You. Amen.

An Encouraged Heart

*"These things I have spoken to you, so that in Me you
may have peace. In the world you have tribulation,
but take courage; I have overcome the world."*
JOHN 16:33 NASB

Gracious and almighty God, I want to walk in Your path of righteousness but so easily get tangled up in the cares of daily life. I live in a fallen world filled with tribulation and heartache. In my feeble attempts to dissuade the causes of my worry, discouragement hovers over me like a dark cloud. The present and future both look bleak. How can I muddle through this despair?

Then You show me the silver lining. "For whatever is born of God overcomes the world; and this is the victory that has overcome the world—our faith" (1 John 5:4 NASB). You have not abandoned me in my trials but have overcome them for me. Gloom and doom are not my destiny. I can have Your peace, which passes all understanding, because of my faith in Your Son, my Lord Jesus Christ. What a wonderful gift of encouragement!

Let me spread this gift through my encouraged heart. As I lift up my face to You in gladness, especially in difficult times, let others see Your promise of peace. Let them see the Son shine within my own sunshine and be encouraged too.

Thank You, heavenly Father, for any opportunity to share the blessings of Your encouragement.

In the name of my precious Lord Jesus, amen.

Down in My Heart

Create in me a pure heart, O God,
and renew a steadfast spirit within me.
PSALM 51:10 NIV

Oh, heavenly Father, what a wonderful gift it is to have Your love embedded so deep in my heart. Nothing is more powerful than the love You have for me. It overcomes all hardship and transgression. Your love fills me up with forgiveness. It washes my heart clean of sin. And when I am downtrodden and weary, it is Your love that refreshes me and gives me the strength to carry on.

I find such peace in Your love, a remarkable peace truly beyond my understanding. When I am troubled, I know that You are there in my heart. I listen and I hear You whisper to me gently, almost like a lullaby, *"Be still, My child. I am here, and I love you."*

You are always here waiting for me in my heart, ready to help me, to comfort and to love me.

And joy! There is such joy in knowing that Your love is eternal. You are with me wherever I go and whatever I do. Nothing can separate me from Your love—nothing at all. In the worst of times, You draw me near to You. You hold me close and love me with a love so pure that there is no mistake that it comes from You.

Oh, thank You, God. Thank You for loving me. Thank You for being there, down in my heart. Amen.

Press On to Know the Lord

*"The LORD is my portion," says my soul, "therefore I will
hope in him." The LORD is good to those who wait for him,
to the soul who seeks him. It is good that one should
wait quietly for the salvation of the LORD.*
LAMENTATIONS 3:24–26 ESV

Lord, I have used Your Word as an owner's manual, only retrieving it from the shelf when I need guidance or comfort. Your words are comfort, but they are more than just a temporary fix; they are a glimpse into Your character. I have heard countless times, "This is God's holy and unerring Word," but do I register what that means? The Bible is Your story, written to reveal Yourself to us through reading and meditating on its content.

My relationship with You has felt stagnant, and I have stopped searching and waiting for You. Once I stop waiting for You, I rely on my own morals, wisdom, and ingenuity to navigate life. These attributes of mine are as useful as an umbrella in a hurricane. The scriptures remind me that You will answer. You are steadfast; it is my unbelief and selfish pride that produce calamity. May my soul seek You; may I press on to know You.

I cannot say that I understand why You have seemingly obscured Your face from me, but I know You will come. I hope in Your constant care and everlasting promises. You are unchanging, and You will answer my cry. Amen.

Come to the Waters

"Come, all you who are thirsty, come to the waters;
and you who have no money, come, buy and eat! Come,
buy wine and milk without money and without cost."
Isaiah 55:1 niv

Dear Father, my spirit feels so dry and thirsty. I long to arrive at a place where I know everything will be all right, where peace and happiness and joy abound, but I'm not sure I'll ever get there. And the more I strive for the things I want, the more elusive they become.

When will I learn to simply rest in You? When will I understand, in the deepest part of me, that I can find everything I need in You? When I'm thirsty, You saturate me. When I'm lonely, You are present. When I'm afraid, You comfort me.

You are my provider. Whether I'm in physical poverty, emotional turmoil, or spiritual destitution, You give me everything I need in abundance. And it's free. For some reason, though, I have trouble trusting You. I forget, so easily, about how good You are.

Help me relax in You today, Lord. When my spirit tightens in worry and stress, remind me of the abundant buffet of Your love, ready and waiting for me to partake. When I'm hungry, fill me. When I'm anxious, give me peace. And when I feel lonely and frightened, comfort me with Your presence. Thank You for loving me, Father. Amen.

Gratitude for God's Love

In this was manifested the love of God toward us, because that God sent his only begotten Son into the world, that we might live through him. Herein is love, not that we loved God, but that he loved us, and sent his Son to be the propitiation for our sins. Beloved, if God so loved us, we ought also to love one another.

1 JOHN 4:9–11 KJV

*L*ord, I worship You for the love You have shown toward me and the world. I've never known such great love as the love You have for Your creation. I'm blessed to receive this wonderful gift. Thank You for loving me when I'm unlovable. Thank You for showing me love when I fail You and neglect our relationship.

I pray for those who have not yet experienced Your love. Man didn't initiate this love; You did. You didn't just speak words but showed us through Your actions how much You care. May they realize the great gift You have given us by sending Your Son to die for them. Open their hearts to receive the love You have for them.

Lord, forgive me for not loving others as I should. Give me a fresh baptism of Your love. Help me love those I feel aren't lovable, those who hurt me and take advantage of me. Let me love, not just in words, but in deeds also. Help me love others as You have loved me. Amen.

God's Blessing

*The LORD bless thee, and keep thee: the LORD make his face
shine upon thee, and be gracious unto thee: the LORD lift
up his countenance upon thee, and give thee peace.*
NUMBERS 6:24–26 KJV

Gracious Lord, when I was a child, that blessing from scripture was proclaimed at the end of each church service. I didn't understand, but it always brought a sense of comfort and a peaceful feeling. It still does. I love to think that You keep me in a special place of blessings where You tenderly care for me and hold me close. I can stay in Your presence and know You will never shove me away.

Your face shines on me, like my mother's when she tucked me in bed at night. I feel Your love. You smile, and a holy light shines from Your face as You look at Your children. I can bask in the light of such love. I feel safe and secure. When You look at me, Your expression covers me with peace like a warm blanket to snuggle in when the world is cold.

Other people may shun me or say hurtful things. They may judge my words or actions. You know me totally, yet You don't sit back, waiting for me to do something stupid so You can wallop me with a rule book. Instead, You are eager to bless me and keep me, to be gracious to me, and to give me peace. What a beautiful promise! Amen.

Trust in Your Loving-Kindness

But I have trusted in Your lovingkindness;
my heart shall rejoice in Your salvation. I will sing
to the LORD, because He has dealt bountifully with me.
PSALM 13:5–6 NASB

Lord, it seems like we're often told to trust in Your strength, or Your sovereignty. To trust in Your loving-kindness is a different but beautiful concept.

Your love is *trustworthy*. Your love never changes. Your love never dwindles. You don't choose to love me based on what I did or did not do for You. You don't remove Your love when I disappoint You. You are never selfish with Your love. Trusting in Your loving-kindness means that I can be absolutely confident that You have my best interests in mind. You will not lead me on the wrong path. The struggles that I am enduring right now are not outside of Your love. When I don't understand how my circumstances could possibly be for my good, I pray that You would give me the faith to simply trust in Your loving-kindness.

Thank You that in Your love You have granted me salvation. This gives my heart so much reason to rejoice, even in the midst of suffering on this earth.

Lord, You have dealt bountifully with me. I praise You now for all the many blessings and wonderful guidance that You have given to me in this life. Amen.

Time for Something New

*"Remember not the former things, nor consider the things
of old. Behold, I am doing a new thing; now it springs
forth, do you not perceive it? I will make a way in
the wilderness and rivers in the desert."*
ISAIAH 43:18–19 ESV

*H*eavenly Father, transition isn't usually easy. You know my past, and when something reminds me of those hurts and old wounds, it can be hard to keep those feelings from coming to the surface. Because of Christ, I have a hope for the future that far surpasses my old stories. I am ready to step into the new season! I can feel it. I know it's coming. Something wonderful and new is out on the horizon. I am in a place today that I have never been. You are with me, and the next thing is almost here.

You have done a new thing in me and for me. I choose today to step out and live each day from here on out in the new. I don't have time to spend in the past. Thank You for giving me a new heart, a new mind, and a new attitude. I want to experience Your love, Your joy, and the excitement of this new adventure with You. You have a vision and plan, and it's slowly unfolding before me. I will embrace what You want to do in me and through me. I will live in the new You have for me, starting now! Amen.

The Heart: Christ's Dwelling Place

So that Christ may dwell in your hearts through faith—that you, being rooted and grounded in love, may have strength to comprehend with all the saints what is the breadth and length and height and depth, and to know the love of Christ that surpasses knowledge, that you may be filled with all the fullness of God.
EPHESIANS 3:17–19 ESV

Father, I bow before You asking that, in the richness of Your glory, You would strengthen my spirit through Your Spirit. Your knowledge, peace, and love go beyond comprehension. Humans are limited in understanding Your beautiful holiness due to our fallen hearts, and yet You still promise us peace that exceeds all possible perception and love that surpasses knowledge.

Dwell in my heart, Messiah, and fill my heart with a strong and joyous trust in You. Root my actions in the sacrificial love of Jesus. Mold my thoughts to have His obedient love as my foundation. Give me, along with the body of Christ in its entirety, the strength to realize Your extensiveness, Your everlasting duration, Your mighty stature, and Your profundity. We will never be able to grasp Your complexity completely. But You revealed to us Your love and personhood through the sacrifice of Jesus so that we may begin to comprehend. Through this journey Your people are guided and filled with the fullness of You. My knowledge is limited, but I trust in Your love, which outshines the sun. Amen.

An Unshakable Heart

Cast your burden upon the LORD and He will sustain you;
He will never allow the righteous to be shaken.
PSALM 55:22 NASB

*D*ear God, we have an enemy, an adversary who wants to shake us up. He is the voice that whispers uncertainties and hopelessness into our hearts. He presses us, in his urgency, to act quickly without considering the consequences. He wants us to be so rattled by our circumstances that we can neither think clearly nor listen for Your calm voice of wisdom.

With Christ as our advocate, we can renounce these irritating distractions. Our Lord takes these burdens from us and confronts and challenges the evil one on our behalf. He proves those uncertainties and hopeless messages are nothing more than ugly lies. Your truth reigns eternally.

As Your children, our trials are temporary. They will come upon us with the regularity of our breathing. But when we rely on Your sustaining love, they will not be allowed to shake us up.

You have promised us an everlasting place in Your unshakable kingdom. "Therefore, since we receive a kingdom which cannot be shaken, let us show gratitude, by which we may offer to God an acceptable service with reverence and awe" (Hebrews 12:28 NASB). Thank You, Father God, for giving us this hope we can cling to in our times of trouble. We will trust in You.

We pray this in the wonderful name of Jesus. Amen.

Don't Send Them Away

Once when some mothers were bringing their children to Jesus to bless them, the disciples shooed them away, telling them not to bother him. But when Jesus saw what was happening he was very much displeased with his disciples and said to them, "Let the children come to me, for the Kingdom of God belongs to such as they. Don't send them away!"

MARK 10:13–14 TLB

*D*ear Jesus, I am guilty of being impatient with my children. When I am stressed out and busy and they want my attention, I react sometimes in an ugly way. I need to remember, Jesus, that they don't understand all the pressure that the world puts on grown-ups. They don't understand why I am harsh with them when I am preoccupied with the business of the world.

You never allowed the world to get in Your way. You always made time for the children. Even when You were busy with huge crowds of people wanting Your attention, You never sent the little ones away.

I want to be like You, Jesus. When I am busy, instead of setting my children aside, I want to bring them near to me. I want to speak kindly and help them understand.

Please forgive me for my impatience. I want to be a mother who is gentle and wise, a mother who understands and makes time for her children, even when the world presses hard against me. Help me, dear Jesus. Amen.

Weight of Your Glory

And the Word became flesh and dwelt among us,
and we have seen his glory, glory as of the only
Son from the Father, full of grace and truth.
JOHN 1:14 ESV

Lord, each day the world shovels more trials on my plate—another bill, sickness, discord in the office or home—and it all drags on my heart. Every emotion tips the scale of my heart, whether the lightness of joy or crushing gravity of sorrow. I am crippled by this burden, and it is not the load of a cumbersome backpack. These worries and desires bind themselves to my mind and heart making mobility near impossible. But the weight of You, Lord, is freedom. Who knew the chains of selfishness could be so heavy and the weight of Christ so light?

Your glory, the weight of Your sacrifice, justice, presence, mercy, grace, and holiness liberates my soul. May I meditate on the sheer wonder that You came down into the world, the one place that hates You, to save me. Nothing else could awaken me to life. I was dead in my transgressions. You traded Your throne to save my decaying heart. Your glory was made manifest through Your Son and His sacrifice. You will not let go of me, nor will You ever relinquish Your grasp. You have shown Your glory. May I take up the weight of You, Lord, and never set it down. Amen.

When I Don't Understand

*"For my thoughts are not your thoughts, neither are your
ways my ways," declares the Lord. "As the heavens are
higher than the earth, so are my ways higher than your
ways and my thoughts than your thoughts."*
Isaiah 55:8–9 niv

*D*ear Father, I want to understand why things happen. When I go through difficult things, I want to know why. But sometimes there doesn't seem to be a reason. Sometimes life just doesn't make sense, and that stresses me out.

When will I learn to trust You, Lord? Though I may not understand my circumstances, You do. You have it all worked out, and You promised to work only for my good. Sometimes I have to go through bad weather to get to a better place.

The problem is, I can only see what's right in front of me. Right here. Right now. And when my current view is glum, I start to feel like that's the only view I'll ever see. I forget that while I can only see today, You've already been to the future and back. You know what's coming. And as Your child, I can relax, knowing You will never lead me into harm.

Remind me today that though I don't know everything, You do. Remind me that I don't have to understand it all. All I have to know is that You are in charge, and You have everything under control. Amen.

God Hears Our Prayers

*And this is the confidence that we have in him, that, if we
ask any thing according to his will, he heareth us: and if
we know that he hear us, whatsoever we ask, we know
that we have the petitions that we desired of him.*
1 JOHN 5:14–15 KJV

Lord, thank You for the confidence we can have when we pray. Your Word tells us we can come to You without doubt, knowing You hear us.

I confess, sometimes I don't pray enough or I ask amiss as the apostle James writes in James 4:3. Confidence comes when I pray according to Your will. I need Your help in this area because sometimes my will wants to take over. Why do I ever think that I know what's best?

Lord, sometimes I get uptight about circumstances and I pray, telling You how to fix the problem. What foolishness on my part. Paul tells us in Philippians 4:6 not to be anxious about anything, but through prayer with thanksgiving to present our petitions to You. Then according to 1 John 5:15, You will hear us and give us whatever we ask.

Father, help me submit to Your will for my life so I can have the confidence to come to You in my time of need. I know You will hear and provide those things that are necessary to take care of the problem. Help me not to ask for foolish things, but only those petitions that please You. Amen.

Divine Rest

If you are tired from carrying heavy burdens, come to me and I will give you rest.
Take the yoke I give you. Put it on your shoulders and learn from me. I am gentle and
humble, and you will find rest. This yoke is easy to bear, and this burden is light.
MATTHEW 11:28–30 CEV

*D*ear Lord, You never ask me to carry a burden that is too heavy. Sometimes I feel like I have more work than I can possibly do or the task is too difficult, and I'm weighed down. I struggle with schedules, my ability, or lack of interest in some project I've agreed to. But if I pause long enough to talk to You about it, I get a different perspective. Have I accepted a responsibility You never expected me to? Did I feel pressured to undertake a venture even though common sense told me not to? Was that Your voice I ignored?

Sometimes when I find myself in situations that wear me down, I can't bow out. I've made a commitment, and if I don't do it, someone else will be overburdened. But when I bring those heavy loads to You, they seem lighter. You can equip me to do more than I feel capable of. You can lead me to another person who is better qualified to do the job and can handle it with ease.

Teach me to come to You before I pick up any burden. Amen.

Delight in the Lord

Delight yourself in the LORD; and He will give you the desires of your heart.
Commit your way to the LORD, trust also in Him, and He will do it. . . .
Rest in the LORD and wait patiently for Him; do not fret because of him who
prospers in his way, because of the man who carries out wicked schemes.
PSALM 37:4–5, 7 NASB

Lord, forgive me when You are not my chief delight. Forgive me when I long for other things more than I long for You. I pray that You would help me find delight in You every day. Open my eyes to Your beauty and Your glory so that I would put You above everything else in my life. Conform my desires to Your will.

I commit my way to You now. I lay down all my anxiety and fear over the plans for the future. I trust that You will make my way clear.

I rest in You, knowing that in Your presence is the safest place I could be. Grant me the patience I need to wait for You to act instead of attempting to take things into my own hands. Thank You that You have promised to take care of me when I trust in You.

Keep me from fretting about all the wickedness in the world. Give me the eternal perspective that You have to remind me that You are ultimately victorious. Amen.

Letting Go of Busyness

Then Jesus said, "Come to me, all of you who are weary
and carry heavy burdens, and I will give you rest."
MATTHEW 11:28 NLT

*L*ord, there are so many good things that I want to be a part of, but I cannot do it all. Today I find myself overcommitted, and I realize I am not spending time with You. Forgive me for letting my priorities get out of whack. When I no longer have the strength to do all the things I've promised, let that be a red flag to me. Wave that flag as a sign that perhaps all that I am doing is not what I *should* be doing. When my to-do list and desire to help others begin to affect my personal relationship with You, then it's time to stop it all. I never want to be too busy to hear You. I need to hear from You every day.

I take time now to get alone with You. I lay all my plans before You. My schedule is Yours to set. Show me what You would have me to do and what things need to come off my plate. Give me courage to let go of the things You don't want me to do today. I will bring my commitments to You before I make them so that I can let You prioritize my life. Above all, I want to please You. Amen.

Anxiety of Separation

When Elisha came into the house, he saw the child
lying dead on his bed. So he went in and shut the door
behind the two of them and prayed to the LORD.
2 KINGS 4:32–33 ESV

God of the living, I cannot imagine the anxiety that must have been in the prophet Elisha's heart to hear that the son You gifted to the faithful Shunammite woman was dead. Losing loved ones is a terror, but it is a heartbreak that can be mended with the comfort of Jesus. He knows what it means to suffer loss. Great Comforter, comfort those who have lost someone dear. For those who are about to experience this separation, prepare their hearts to look to You for peace. In times of sickness and death, keep the hearts of Your people stayed on You.

Just as Elisha had the example of Elijah before him (who also prayed for the son who died of the sacrificial widow from Zarephath!), so believers today have faithful warriors of the past as an encouragement. Through heart-wrenching difficulties they continued to see Your grace. Ultimately You are our portion and our sustenance, and we look to You for healing. Adonai, King of kings, thank You for hearing Elisha's prayer by giving life back to the child. However, many do not experience healing in this world. Help all to know complete healing and comfort whether in this life or in the life to come through Jesus' victory over death. Amen.

A Humble Heart

Search me, O God, and know my heart; try me and know
my anxious thoughts; and see if there be any hurtful
way in me, and lead me in the everlasting way.
PSALM 139:23–24 NASB

*H*eavenly Father, I come to You in prayer, asking You to search me, to know my heart and my anxious thoughts. But You do know them. You have known me since before I was born. I bring You no surprises, especially in difficult times.

I ask You to search my heart for my own sake, to show me my hurtful ways. When stress and strife bear down on me, I don't see how insensitive I am to others' needs.

Seeing the results of Your mighty yet tender hand moving within my circumstances is humbling. It often brings me to my knees before Your throne of glory. I am helpless to overcome my plight without Your divine intervention, which often includes the help of loved ones, friends, or strangers. My pride gets in the way, and I push them away.

Only in humility can I look beyond my anxious thoughts to see how I hurt others who cross my path. Then I must pray, "Create in me a clean heart, O God, and renew a steadfast spirit within me" (Psalm 51:10 NASB).

Search me, try me, help me, Lord. With a clean and humble heart, I can follow Your lead into the way of everlasting love.

I pray this in Jesus' name. Amen.

Prayer for a Broken Heart

In her deep anguish Hannah prayed to the Lord,
weeping bitterly. . . . As she kept on praying to the Lord,
Eli observed her mouth. Hannah was praying in her heart,
and her lips were moving but her voice was not heard.
1 Samuel 1:10, 12–13 niv

Dear God, my heart is broken. Sadness overwhelms me. There are no other feelings but sadness, so deep and intense. How long, Father? How long will I feel so shattered and lost?

Friends and family try to help me. They attempt to fill up the hollowness inside me with their kindness and love. And while I appreciate them, Father, and all that they do, nothing can fill up the emptiness—nothing but You.

Night and day, I cry out to You. Tears fall hot upon my cheeks, and I know that You see them. I know that You hear me and You understand. You will see me through this, Father. I believe that You will. But right now, today, I need You to comfort me.

When I have no words with which to pray, then hear the Holy Spirit praying for me. Bind up my wounded heart with Your gentle love, and bathe me with Your comforting presence. Shine Your light into my darkness and lead me out of this valley.

Oh, Lord. You are the Great Healer, the mender of broken hearts. Come to me, Father. Come to me now, and fill me up with You! Amen.

What God Requires

"With what shall I come before the LORD, and bow myself before God on high? Shall I come before him with burnt offerings, with calves a year old?" . . . He has told you, O man, what is good; and what does the LORD require of you but to do justice, and to love kindness, and to walk humbly with your God?

MICAH 6:6, 8 ESV

Lord, when my heart is calloused and cold, only Your Word, voice, and Spirit can heal. The God of the universe reaches down and breathes life into my heart. Salvation, creation, and this life have never been about me. What does the God of the universe require of me, a sinner? He requires me to do justice, love kindness, and walk humbly with Him.

Lord, I confess I have seldom performed any of those actions, and when I have it has not been with my whole heart as You desire and deserve. I recall those times that I meditated on Your glory and grace, and joy filled my soul. All things pale in comparison to the loveliness and beauty of Your presence. To walk humbly with You is a lifetime honor and eternal delight, which You have bestowed upon me. Lord, forgive me for taking my relationship with You for granted. In these frantic times when I wonder what action to take, may I recall Your word to do justice, love kindness, and walk with You humbly. May I never see the goodness or pain in my life as my own work; all of it comes from You and all of it is in Your control. I am in Your arms. Amen.

A Beautiful Place

"You will go out in joy and be led forth in peace; the mountains and hills will burst into song before you, and all the trees of the field will clap their hands. Instead of the thornbush will grow the juniper, and instead of briers the myrtle will grow. This will be for the Lord's renown, for an everlasting sign, that will endure forever."
ISAIAH 55:12–13 NIV

*D*ear Father, thank You for the beautiful promises found in this verse. Each part of it thrills my heart. I will go out in joy. One of these days, joy will fill my life. I can picture it now, with me laughing and smiling all the way down to my soul.

I will be led forth in peace. All the strife and turmoil, all the broken relationships and painful associations will one day be mended, and my heart won't feel so swollen with sadness. One day, love will wipe out the strife and anger and bitterness, and there will be a gentle understanding among the people who hold my heart. There will be peace.

Lord, much of my life seems like briers and thornbushes. But You promised juniper and sweet-smelling, colorful myrtle. The resulting joy and peace pouring from my life will be a sign, pointing others to You.

Father, I'm ready. I'm ready for that joy and peace. I'm ready for the thorns and briers to be replaced with juniper and myrtle. I trust You. My hope is in You. Thank You for working in my life to bring me to that beautiful place. Amen.

Joy Comes in the Morning

For his anger endureth but a moment; in his favour is life:
weeping may endure for a night, but joy cometh in the morning. . . .
Thou hast turned for me my mourning into dancing: thou
hast put off my sackcloth, and girded me with gladness.
PSALM 30:5, 11 KJV

Lord, it's hard to feel joy in the middle of pain. Grief and anguish can blind me to the fact that You're in control and this heartbreak won't last forever. Nights can be terribly long when I can't see through the darkness surrounding my world.

Forgive me, Lord, when I allow myself to be blinded by trials, when I forget that You are my burden bearer. Sometimes I become self-centered and can't think of anyone but myself and what I'm feeling. I know self-pity is displeasing to You. I repent of these selfish feelings and ask for spiritual eyesight to see that others are suffering also.

Help me remember that in You I have life, and that life can be lived in the light even though darkness threatens my feeling of well-being. Tears come to everyone at times, and my life is no exception, but Your Word promises joy will come in the morning. You will turn these tears into rejoicing and fill me with gladness.

Nothing feels quite like the joy You place in our hearts. It banishes the darkness and self-pity. It places a song of praise on my lips. Thank You, Lord, for joy in the morning. Amen.

The Love God Wants

The person who has My commands and keeps them is the one who [really] loves Me; and whoever [really] loves Me will be loved by My Father, and I [too] will love him and will show (reveal, manifest) Myself to him. [I will let Myself be clearly seen by him and make Myself real to him.]

JOHN 14:21 AMPC

What do You look for in people who really love You, Lord? I know we don't have to earn Your love—we can't—You love us unconditionally. You say the person who loves You keeps Your commandments. I can recite the Ten Commandments, but they make me stumble sometimes. I would never admit that I have other gods, but sometimes I allow trivial things to control my life. I choose what I can do by how much it costs or how much time it will take. Have I made money or my schedule a god?

I confess that I don't keep the Sabbath holy, sometimes I envy others, and I've lied more than I want to admit. Thank You that those things don't make You give up on me, but I desperately want to show the love You look for. I know it's more than merely doing *things*.

You ask for my whole life. When I am totally Yours, I will do what You ask me to do just because I love to make You happy. I give You everything that matters to me, Lord. Amen.

Never Forsaken

The steps of a man are established by the Lord, and He delights in his way. When he falls, he will not be hurled headlong, because the Lord is the One who holds his hand. I have been young and now I am old, yet I have not seen the righteous forsaken or his descendants begging bread.

PSALM 37:23–25 NASB

Lord, You have established my steps. I am not wandering through this life aimlessly or on my own. You have planned exactly where I will go. And You delight in seeing me follow Your path. It is remarkable that You would delight in my little life. What value my life has knowing that You rejoice in it. Help me be a reflection of Your delight and glory to those around me.

Thank You that You keep me from falling. You hold me up so that, even when I feel that I have hit rock bottom, You are still underneath me to support me and pick me back up onto my feet. May I lean ever more on You, knowing that You are there right beside me through every step I take.

Thank You, Lord, for this testimony that You do not ever forsake Your children. You will never leave me or forget about me. Even if everyone else were to leave me, You would still be my Father and Friend. There is no one and nothing that could separate You from me. Amen.

Make Time to Laugh

A joyful heart is good medicine,
but a crushed spirit dries up the bones.
PROVERBS 17:22 ESV

Jesus, the Bible says You were God and man. I believe You experienced all the emotions I experience—including joy, which produces laughter. I can imagine You laughing and joking with Your friends with a sense of lightheartedness and fun. Life can be all too serious sometimes. I guess I take myself too seriously and can forget to experience joy and laughter. Life can be stressful, but a light heart can help ease the tension and allow for difficult moments to become less trying. Help me lighten up and live a little louder with more laughter.

Forgive me for missing those opportunities to laugh with friends and family, or to even laugh at myself. You give me opportunities to spend time with friends and share joy with one another. Sometimes I'm too focused on work or busyness and I miss the joy that is happening around me. Open my eyes to see the funnier side of situations. May I add to the life of others with a joyful heart, instead of sucking the life out of them with negative words.

Speak to my heart and help me see the world through humorous lenses. Teach me about Your sense of humor. Give me glimpses in Your Word to see how Your joy and laughter spilled out onto others. Amen.

Weapons of God's Might

For the weapons of our warfare are not of the flesh but have divine power to destroy strongholds. We destroy arguments and every lofty opinion raised against the knowledge of God, and take every thought captive to obey Christ.

2 CORINTHIANS 10:4–5 ESV

Prince of Peace, teach me how to be prepared for battle in this world. Believers get caught up in stress and rely on frail human resources to combat fear and fretfulness. Forgive me for relying on my supposed strength, which is in fact weakness. I dwell on my concerns and situations without the sword of the Spirit to parry doubts.

Gird me with the belt of truth to have Jesus as the way, the truth, and the light always surrounding my thoughts and actions. Let the breastplate of righteousness received through faith in Jesus protect me against thoughts of self-righteousness or thoughts of worthlessness. I am made worthy to enter into Your presence by the righteous blood of Jesus.

Make me wear the shoes of the Gospel of peace to walk as one reconciled with my Creator and spreading the Good News of reconciliation. Let me take up constantly the shield of faith to protect against the deceptions of the devil. Crown me with the helmet of salvation to know I am Yours and You are mine forever.

Your armor has the power to destroy the most oppressive strongholds. I bring every worry to You. Then my anxious heart knows Your peace, which guards my heart and mind in Christ. Amen.

An Open Heart

*"Ask, and it will be given to you; seek, and you will find;
knock, and it will be opened to you."*
MATTHEW 7:7 NASB

*L*ord God, my troubling thoughts feel like a full-scale attack. I pull inside myself like a shrinking violet. When I implode in despair, I trap those anxieties inside with me. I can escape them only if I open myself back up. You help me do this with Your Word.

When I pray, *open my eyes to see Your wondrous miracles.* You point me to Psalm 119:18 (NASB)—"Open my eyes, that I may behold wonderful things from Your law." Understanding Your Word gives me a heavenly viewpoint.

Open my ears to hear Your words of encouragement. You respond with: " 'He opens their ear to instruction, and commands that they return from evil' " (Job 36:10 NASB). You allow some trials to get my attention.

Open my mouth to praise You, knowing You are near. Then I find: "O Lord, open my lips, that my mouth may declare Your praise" (Psalm 51:15 NASB).

Open my heart to accept Your will. You show me Your love with: " 'How much more will your Father who is in heaven give what is good to those who ask Him!' " (Matthew 7:11 NASB).

I ask You for help. You are here. I seek Your solutions. You reveal them. I knock at Your door in faith. You open it.

With my heart open to You, Lord, I can release my trouble and accept Your peace. Amen.

A Perfectionist's Prayer

Nothing is completely perfect, except your teachings.
PSALM 119:96 CEV

*D*ear heavenly Father, I admit that I am a perfectionist. I am guilty of thinking that everything I do has to be perfect—and I am also guilty of believing that I *can* be perfect! I carry that load of perfectionism with me every day, and I add to it the burden of anxiety that comes with being imperfect. I confess to You, Father, that I have been trying so hard to achieve perfection that I have forgotten that no one can be perfect, except You.

I am not like You that everything I do should be flawlessly complete and whole. Please help me remember that. Remind me that my imperfection is a gift because it teaches me to rely on You and to be in awe of Your greatness. Show me that there is a difference between doing my best to please You and striving to be perfect to please myself.

Father, forgive me. My focus has been on how I want others to perceive me. I have made every effort to be first in all that I do instead of making every effort to focus on doing my best for You. I am nothing without You.

Lord, teach me to be satisfied with my imperfection. Help me embrace it, knowing that You love me just the way that I am. And help me love myself, imperfections and all. Amen.

The Lord Blessed

*The LORD blessed the latter part of
Job's life more than the former part.*
JOB 42:12 NIV

*D*ear Father, it's hard not to be anxious about the future. Sometimes I worry what will happen this afternoon; other times I get bogged down with what will become of me when I'm old and can no longer care for myself. But when I look at Job's life, I'm reminded that You are all about happy endings.

I'm certain I will walk through some difficult days, just as Job did. I also know that You will never leave me. Even in the midst of unbearable circumstances, I can have peace, knowing You're still writing my story. The difficult moments only serve to strengthen my character and to make the good times even sweeter.

Right now I'm going through some hard times, Lord. Things aren't the way I want them to be. And I wish I could fast-forward through this season and get to a better place. But I'm sure You have me here for a reason, to teach me something. And I know this isn't the end of the story.

You are the same yesterday, today, and tomorrow. Just as You carried Job through difficult times and poured out Your goodness on him at the end of his trials, I know You'll do the same for me. There will be a day, sometime soon, when You will bless me more than I've ever been blessed before. And when it's all said and done, I'll spend eternity with You, which will be the greatest blessing of all. Amen.

Trust in the Lord

In you, LORD, I have taken refuge; let me never be put to shame;
deliver me in your righteousness. Turn your ear to me, come quickly to my
rescue; be my rock of refuge, a strong fortress to save me. Since you are
my rock and my fortress, for the sake of your name lead and guide me.
PSALM 31:1–3 NIV

Lord, as I watch the news and hear the reports of tragedy and calamity around the world, I feel anxious about the future. What is going to happen next? Will my family be affected? Who can we trust and depend on in this time of chaos? Then I remember Your Word.

Thank You, Lord, for the words of comfort I find in the Bible. I can take refuge in You and the promises You have given me. I know there is nothing in the future that You can't handle. You already know what lies ahead and You have made provision for Your people. All I have to do is call and You will come to my rescue.

Lord, I pray that You will help me put everything into Your hands. When I hear frightening news reports, hear about the injustice endured by innocent people, and see devastation of entire cities, help me remember that You are my rock of refuge. You are my fortress. You will strengthen me for the days ahead. Whatever I face, You will be there. Thank You for this comfort and protection. Amen.

Trust Fund

*"Blessed is the man who trusts in the L*ord *and whose trust
is the L*ord*. For he will be like a tree planted by the water,
that extends its roots by a stream and will not fear when the
heat comes; but its leaves will be green, and it will not be
anxious in a year of drought nor cease to yield fruit."*
Jeremiah 17:7–8 nasb

Dear Father, right now I feel like I'm in a drought. Like a tree without water, I'm afraid I'm going to dry up, wither away and die. And yet, during this time of drought, You want me to just relax and trust You.

Father, this verse promises that if I trust You, even when it's hard, I'll flourish. I'll be like a tree planted by water. I know You are the living water, and when I'm connected to You, I have all the life and nourishment I need to prosper and bear good fruit.

Not only am I supposed to trust You, but my trust is supposed to be in You. The wording is a little confusing until I think of it like a trust fund. I'm placing my trust in You, knowing that trust will grow and produce good things that will benefit me and the people around me.

When I trust You, I choose to believe in Your goodness. When my trust is in You, I invest in my relationship with You, knowing it will always produce a healthy return. Thank You, Father, for Your love. I know I will flourish, even in hard times, because I've placed my trust in You. Amen.

Strength and Protection

*But the Lord can be trusted to make
you strong and protect you from harm.*
2 THESSALONIANS 3:3 CEV

Thank You, my faithful Father, that You are trustworthy in every way. Thank You for making me strong and protecting me from harm. Satan wants to destroy those who follow You. But You invite me to abide in You (John 15:4), where I can stay totally safe.

You promise never to leave me, but sometimes I wander off, doing my own thing. When I'm unaware of Your presence, I become vulnerable. I can be deceived by temptations along the way and lose sight of the really important opportunities to accomplish what You want. Then I fall into dangerous territory.

I long to stay so close to You that I hear Your voice. When You whisper, I want to be ready to listen and obey. Then I will glorify You with the fruit our relationship produces. I long to stay so close to You all the time that my heart beats like Yours, with compassion for those who need You. Then I will be strong and prepared to do Your will, going where You tell me to go, doing what You tell me to do. And people will see You in my life.

My heart's desire is to trust in Your provisions, doing everything You have planned for me. Keep me in the place You have prepared for me, where I am safe and equipped to do Your will. Amen.

He Gives Strength to the Weary

Do you not know? Have you not heard? The Everlasting God, the Lord, the Creator of the ends of the earth does not become weary or tired. His understanding is inscrutable. He gives strength to the weary, and to him who lacks might He increases power. . . . Yet those who wait for the Lord will gain new strength; they will mount up with wings like eagles, they will run and not get tired, they will walk and not become weary.

ISAIAH 40:28–29, 31 NASB

Lord, You are the everlasting God, the Creator of the universe. You are never tired or weary. You are always alert and always full of power.

I, on the other hand, am often tired and weary. I don't always know if I can keep going and push through another day.

But You offer me strength, and You offer it to me in abundance. You have endless power to offer, so why do I so often try to make it on my own? Forgive me when I forget that You have promised to give strength to Your children.

I will rest in You and wait for You to grant me new strength so that I might mount up with wings like eagles. Give me the endurance and perseverance to run the race of life. And when I feel like I can go no farther, I trust that You will be there to pick me up and give me the strength I need for one more day. Amen.

His Love Overcomes Disappointment

And this hope will never disappoint us, because God has poured out his love to fill our hearts. He gave us his love through the Holy Spirit, whom God has given to us.
ROMANS 5:5 NCV

God, disappointment can feel like I swallowed a rock. It sits there in my stomach, heavy and painful. It weighs on my emotions and can sometimes make me physically ill. I am disappointed in myself setting unrealistic expectations for others. Even when they say they will but don't meet the standard I set, I allow them to disappoint me. Help me be realistic about what others promise or what I have the ability to do myself.

Your love never disappoints me. You have given me a hope that will never wane. It may not look like I imagined, but I can trust that Your plans will always turn out to be Your very best for me. When disappointment comes to destroy my dreams and shatter my hope, I will focus on You and continue to believe Your promises. You alone can give me hope that does not disappoint. Fill me with Your joy; let it bubble over into all my world. I receive Your love. May it consume my heart and fill any void disappointment can bring. Life can bring disappointment, but I have Your promised hope for blessing. You are the One who can make my dreams a reality. I put all my hope in You! Amen.

God Is My Portion

My flesh and my heart may fail, but God is the
strength of my heart and my portion forever.
PSALM 73:26 NIV

God, You know that I have done all that I can do. It is not possible for me to fix this situation. I am left only to put all my faith and my trust in You. You alone know the outcome. You are the only One who knows what to do. So I call on You now for help: help me, please, to be strong. Help me to wait peacefully, knowing that You are my portion—You are enough.

Father, when I doubt, then increase my portion of faith. Give me an ocean of assurance. When hope is just a knoll in this valley, then increase my portion and grow the hill into a mountain. And when my trust in You fades, then fill up my heart with Your light, overflowing.

You are my portion, Father. You are enough. You know exactly what I need. You know when I need it, and how much. You provide generously, always, without fail. So why do I worry? Why am I afraid when You are my hope? You are the strength of my heart, and Your provision is always enough.

I call on You now to help me. Please bring me through this situation and into the shining light of Your love. Give me peace in knowing that You are my portion—You are enough. Amen.

God Gives the Increase

I planted the seed, Apollos watered it, but God has been making it grow. So neither the one who plants nor the one who waters is anything, but only God, who makes things grow. The one who plants and the one who waters have one purpose, and they will each be rewarded according to their own labor.

1 Corinthians 3:6–8 niv

Lord, sometimes I feel I'm not accomplishing anything with all the work I do. It seems as if I'm spinning my wheels. I feel weary with the sameness of what I do. I know I shouldn't worry about the end results, but if I can't see anything happening, how will I know to continue?

I confess, Lord, that I'm one of those who want to see the finished product of my work. Forgive me for worrying about whether I see the end result. Paul said he had planted the seed and Apollos watered it, but You are the one who gave the increase to the work they started. Lord, give me the same spirit Paul had—that we are nothing. It's You who gives life to the seeds we plant.

Thank You, Lord, for the opportunity to work for You. Thank You for the purpose You give to my labors. Give me a willing spirit and keep me from feeling weary of well-doing. Lord, help me not to worry what others are accomplishing for You, but be diligent about the job You've given me. Amen.

Contributors

Jean Fischer, a former Golden Books editor, has been writing for children for nearly three decades. She lives in Racine, Wisconsin. Jean's prayers can be found on pages: 12, 21, 30, 39, 50, 59, 70, 79, 88, 97, 106, 115, 124, 133, 142, 151, 160, 169, 178, 185

Renae Brumbaugh Green lives in Texas with two noisy children and two dogs. She's authored four books in Barbour's Camp Club Girls series. Renae's prayers can be found on pages: 14, 23, 32, 41, 52, 61, 63, 72, 81, 90, 99, 108, 117, 126, 144, 153, 162, 171, 179, 181

Shanna D. Gregor is a freelance writer, editor, and product developer who has served various ministries and publishers. The mother of two young men, Shanna resides with her husband in Tucson, Arizona. Shanna's prayers can be found on pages: 9, 18, 27, 36, 47, 56, 67, 76, 85, 94, 103, 112, 121, 130, 139, 148, 157, 166, 175, 184

Ardythe Kolb writes articles and devotions for various publications and is currently working on her third book. She serves on the advisory board of a writers' network and edits their newsletter. Ardythe's prayers can be found on pages: 7, 16, 25, 34, 45, 54, 65, 74, 83, 92, 101, 110, 119, 128, 137, 146, 155, 164, 173, 182

Emily Marsh lives in Virginia with her husband, Seth, and their various pit bull foster puppies. She works at a downtown real estate firm as a client care coordinator and teaches ballet in her spare time. Emily's prayers can be found on pages: 8, 17, 26, 35, 46, 55, 66, 75, 84, 93, 102, 111, 120, 129, 138, 147, 156, 165, 174, 183

Lydia Mindling is inspired to write by three things: God's love, Christ's sacrifice, and creation. When not writing, Lydia enjoys horseback riding, hikes, and attempts at baking the world's best brownies. Lydia's prayers can be found on pages: 13, 22, 31, 40, 43, 51, 60, 64, 71, 80, 89, 98, 107, 116, 125, 134, 143, 152, 161, 170

Vickie Phelps lives in East Texas with her husband, Sonny, and their schnauzer, Dobber. She divides her time between family, writing, and church activities. Vickie's prayers can be found on pages: 15, 24, 33, 42, 53, 62, 73, 82, 91, 100, 109, 118, 127, 135, 145, 154, 163, 172, 180, 186

Iemima Ploscariu is a history researcher who spends most of her time in Sacramento, California. She holds an MLitt in Central and Eastern European history and is pursuing further studies. Along with her freelance writing, she also serves in the children's and women's ministries of her local Romanian church. Iemima's prayers can be found on pages: 10, 19, 28, 37, 48, 57, 68, 77, 86, 95, 104, 113, 122, 131, 136, 140, 149, 158, 167, 176

Janet Ramsdell Rockey is a freelance Christian writer living in Tampa, Florida, with her Realtor husband and two cats. Janet's prayers can be found on pages: 11, 20, 29, 38, 44, 49, 58, 69, 78, 87, 96, 105, 114, 123, 132, 141, 150, 159, 168, 177

Try the Original Devotional!

Prayers for an Anxious Heart

Dozens of practical and encouraging prayers inspired by Philippians 4:6–7 will help women of all ages strengthen their heart-connection to the Master Creator. Readers will discover a deeper understanding and love for the One who holds the whole world in His hands.

DiCarta / 978-1-68322-171-5 / $12.99